FULL MOON

FULL MOON

AND OTHER PLAYS

Reynolds Price

Theatre Communications Group

1993

Full Moon and Other Plays is published by Theatre Communications Group, Inc., 355 Lexington Ave., New York, NY 10017.

Price, Reynolds, 1933–
Full moon and other plays / Reynolds Price.—1st ed.
Contents: Early dark—Private contentment—Full moon.
ISBN 1-55936-063-1 (cloth)—ISBN 1-55936-064-X (paper)
I. Title
PS3566.R54F84 1993
812'.54—dc20 92-44383
CIP

Book design by The Sarabande Press
Cover design by Cynthia Krupat
Type composition by The Typeworks
First Edition, March 1993

CONTENTS

EARLY DARK

FOR

KATHLEEN & HARRY FORD

This play shares plot with a novel called *A Long and Happy Life*, which tells an earlier version of similar events in the lives of a few Americans in the summer, fall and winter of 1957. The playwright shares the novelist's name and some of his physical and mental traits. He is changed however, by nineteen years.

Thus the play is not the novel dramatized. It is rather the same general set of actions, the same few people seen by a different man who stands elsewhere and sees otherwise. The story of the play differs therefore from the novel's as two alert but separate witnesses' versions of a complex event will inevitably and instructively differ. Comparisons may be made and one version may ultimately prove more useful; but whatever their effects and fates, both stories were told in need and pleasure, in the hope they would cause need and pleasure in others—needs not satisfied by stories alone, whatever their forms.

The story occurs in Warren County in northeastern North Carolina; but while that scene has shaped the people, it has not deformed them; and its characteristics should not be exploited for quaintness or humor, color or patronage. Such people could tell Sophocles or Beckett numerous complicated facts and possibilities.

Stage-Southern accents, gestures and clothing should be avoided or powerfully restrained. The South is larger than—and linguistically as various as—New England, the Mid-Atlantic and a large piece of the Midwest combined. There are almost as many Southern accents as Southerners; and in nearly forty years of play- and moviegoing, I have never heard a non-Southern actor produce one with more than modest accuracy (decamped Southerners frequently offer grievous parodies). A generally non-urban American accent and rhythm is recommended when the play is produced outside its native county.

The clothes are those of upper working-class America of the early '50s (fashion taking a few years then to work its way South).

Any music would derive from church or popular radio—no straight hair and dulcimers. Pervasive country sounds would help—the steady chorus of birds, crickets, frogs till October silence. Vehicle sounds should be carefully controlled; motorcycle noise should be barely indicated if used at all.

Fluidity of progress should be the first aim of set design. There should be a minimum of pauses (within acts only five pauses are implied, and skill might eliminate several of those; scene numbers indicate substantial shifts of time or place). Three physical areas appear necessary, in my mind at least—stage left, the Mustian house (two rooms required, Rosacoke's upstairs); a central all-purpose out-of-doors; and stage right, all other places (the two churches, Mary's, Wesley's, Mr. Isaac's; the lake can lie behind the audience, aisles being used for running swimmers—and in Act Three for the pageant processions). There may be more effective solutions, but a slow set will be bad.

The two church services—black funeral, white pageant—are main supports to the arc of the action: the chief opportunities for ritual expression by different but inextricable races. They must be staged in their urgent solemnity, dignity and fervor. Costumes for the pageant are simple oddments from family closets, none comic. A touch of condescension will poison both rites and hide the burning target of these lives.

The play can be shown in many right ways. The only wrong way would start by forgetting that the story of the species is mostly lived out in huts, houses, woods, fields—far from towns and cities. These people move with the weight of that certainty, the tragic glee of the well-informed.

Stuart White, Howard Ashman and Kyle Renick gave this play a first and beautiful production at the WPA Theatre in the spring of 1978. It was a grand time for all of us, no one foreseeing that Stuart would be one of the first to die of AIDS nor that Howard would follow him in 1991. In this new edition of the text the three of them brought to startling life, I thank them again profoundly—Stuart and Howard in death, Kyle still at his work.

R.P., *1993*

CHARACTERS

WHITE

EMMA MUSTIAN - *a widow, 45, housekeeper for her children*
MILO - *Emma's son, 24, a tobacco farmer*
RATO - *Emma's son, 22, an Army corporal; his name is pronounced Ray-toe*
ROSACOKE - *Emma's daughter, 20, a telephone operator. Burdened by vision and intelligence but the credible object of a young man's care*
BABY SISTER - *Emma's daughter, 11, a sixth-grade student*
SISSIE - *Milo's wife, 22, idle*
WESLEY BEAVERS - *local boy, 22, a cycle salesman. Magnetic in stillness, with the air of power abiding its time*
WILLIE DUKE AYCOCK - *local girl, 22, a beautician*
MACEY GUPTON - *local farmer, 25*
MARISE - *Macey's wife and mother of three, 24*
ISAAC ALSTON - *local landowner, 86, half-paralyzed*
MR. MASON - *proprietor of Mason's Lake, a Free Will Baptist preacher, 48*
HEYWOOD BETTS - *scrap-metal merchant from Newport News, Va., 34*
REV. VEREEN - *of Delight Baptist Church, young to middle-aged (unseen)*
DR. SLEDGE - *local physician, 60 (silent)*

SHEPHERDS - *three to five adolescent boys (silent)*
CHOIR - *three to four male and/or female voices*

BLACK

MRS. RANSOM - *Sammy Ransom's mother, 46, a church leader*
REV. MINGIE - *of Mount Moriah Church, middle-aged to old*
MARY SUTTON - *dead Mildred's mother, 37, an occasional housemaid*
SAMMY RANSOM - *Mr. Isaac Alston's man, 22*

PLACES

Warren County, North Carolina and Mason's Lake, Virginia

TIME

Summer, fall and winter 1957

SCENES

Act One

1. *The Mustian place*
2. *Mount Moriah Church*
3. *Mr. Isaac Alston's woods*
4. *Mason's Lake*

Act Two

1. *The Mustian place*
2. *Mary Sutton's house*
3. *Wesley's house and the woods, the Mustian place*

Act Three

1. *The Mustian dining room*
2. *The same, Mr. Isaac Alston's place*
3. *Delight Church*
4. *Delight churchyard*

ACT ONE

1

Warren County, North Carolina; a small tobacco farm; a Sunday morning in late July 1957.

On a downstairs porch of the Mustian home, Baby Sister, Sissie and Milo wait hot and dark.

In an upstairs bedroom Emma Mustian sits dressed on the bed. Her daughter Rosacoke faces the window, wearing only her white slip.

EMMA

Why?

ROSACOKE

He's what I want.

EMMA

Why?

ROSACOKE

He's always been.

EMMA

The world's full of people—

ROSACOKE

Not for me.

EMMA

Since when?

ROSACOKE

(Still at the window, facing out; realizing as she goes) Seven years this November. You had punished me for laughing that morning in church, and I wanted to die—which was nothing unusual—but guessed I could live if I breathed a little air, so I picked up a bucket and walked to the woods to hunt some nuts and win you back. It was getting on late. I was hoping you were worried. I was past Mr. Isaac's in the really deep woods. The leaves were all gone, but I hadn't found a nut. Still I knew of one tree Mildred Sutton had showed me—I was headed for that—and I found it finally. It was loaded—pecans the size of sparrows—and in the top fork a boy, a stranger to me. I was not even scared. He seemed to live there, twenty yards off the ground, staring out dead-level. I said "Are you strong enough to shake your tree?" —"If I wanted to," he said. I said "Well, want to please; I'm standing here hungry." He thought and then braced his long legs and arms and rocked four times—pecans nearly killed me. I rummaged round and filled my bucket, my pockets. He had still not faced me; so I said "Don't you want to share some of my pecans?" Then he looked down and smiled and said "I heard they were God's." I said "No, really they belong to Mr. Isaac Alston. He can't see this far." —"I can see him," he said. "You may can see Philadelphia," I said—he was looking back north—and he nodded to that but didn't look down. "How old are you?" I said. He said "Fifteen" and shut up again. "I'm thirteen," I said. He said "You'll live" and smiled once more toward Philadelphia and I came on home. I wanted him then and every day since.

EMMA

You're saying that's a reason to ruin your day?

ROSACOKE

Yes ma'm—my life.

Milo steps from the porch to the yard, looks up, speaks to Rosa's window.

MILO

You're a fool and you know it. Just as well lie there and wait for snow.

Emma starts downstairs.

MILO

You'd think Wesley Beavers was General MacArthur—everybody waiting in July sun while he decides to come or stay. What the hell did he say anyhow?

BABY SISTER

Nothing as usual. His mother called Rosacoke Friday night, said Wesley was being discharged on Saturday and would be here to see her by Saturday night.

MILO

Yeah. Well, this is Sunday and the picnic is melting. Rosa, haul your simple self down here!

EMMA

(In the door) Milo, hush. What have you ever waited on in your life for more than two minutes?

MILO

I've been waiting six months for my baby boy.

SISSIE

It's half my baby and it may be a girl.

MILO

We've all been waiting—what is it? three years—for Wesley to sail home for good from the Navy and put a smile back on Weeping Willow's face. Last call, Rosa!

EMMA

I told you to hush. She's dressing now. Didn't you hear her walking past midnight, staring at the road?

MILO

No, I sleep when it's dark. Well, I mostly sleep. *(Grins toward Sissie)*

SISSIE

Are we leaving now and stirring a breeze or am I getting sick?

BABY SISTER

Me too.

EMMA

Be ashamed, all of you. Just shut up and wait. If that girl turned against any one of you, you'd lose your best friend. *(Looks to Rosa's window)* Rosa, listen to reason. He'll come in good time—he grew up here; he'll track you down. He doesn't run his own life; show him you run yours. *(Listens for an answer)* Are you coming, Rosa?

ROSACOKE

I'm coming.

MILO

Praise Jesus! Her Highness is going to favor us, huh?

EMMA

Your sister is coming if that's what you mean; and if you speak one hard word to her now, you can leave my house. It's mine till I die.

They are stopped by the distant roar of a motorcycle.

SISSIE

Is this it?

BABY SISTER

Who else?

Rosa appears at her window unsmiling; then quickly pulls inward as the roar increases, stops.

Wesley enters—white shirt, khaki trousers, plain brown shoes. No one greets him.

WESLEY

All you need to say is "Welcome back to freedom." *(Silence still so he turns to Milo)* You never spent three years in a sailor suit, so you don't know how happy I am.

MILO

I've spent nineteen years staring up a mule's ass. I've spent three years watching my next sister wait around for you. We've all spent this morning watching her wait—and last night too. It's held us up from the church picnic, and Rosacoke all but missed the funeral.

WESLEY

What funeral, Mrs. Mustian?

EMMA

Mildred Sutton died Friday. Colored Mildred, Mary's child—you remember Mildred.

MILO

Having somebody's baby, some unknown father.

EMMA

Rosa grew up with Mildred and kept up with her. Still she was ready to miss Mildred's funeral because of you.

WESLEY

I never heard a word about a death. I got my discharge noon yesterday and have come one hundred and thirty miles, not stopping, this morning to see Rosacoke—haven't even been home. That's the best I could do.

MILO

Noon yesterday was a whole day ago. Where you been so long?

WESLEY

Settling things.

MILO

What waters were troubled? Who you been stirring up?

EMMA

Milo, put this food—and Sissie—in the car. They're cooking too fast. *(Turns to Wesley, yielding now, though Milo doesn't move)* Well, you're back home now. We can all make adjustments.

WESLEY

Just today and tonight.

EMMA

Where then?

WESLEY

Back to Norfolk in the morning. Got a good job in Norfolk, selling motorcycles. I'm here to see Rosa.

EMMA

That's news to us. We thought you'd be back here farming for your father.

WESLEY

No ma'm. I decided my chance is in Norfolk.

EMMA

I'm sorry, Wesley. I know your mother's sorry.

Wesley smiles and nods.

MILO

Sorry?—for what? That this boy here is running off again? We all ought to thank the good old Lord—ought to fall on our knees right now and say "Thank you, Lord, for sparing our family by taking this troublemaker out of our midst. Now give us some sleep."

WESLEY

Don't thank Him too soon. Norfolk's not round the world.

Rosa stands at the front door in white, a wide summer hat; walks to the porch steps and smiles down at Wesley.

He smiles in reply; quickly finds a harmonica; and plays "Home, Sweet Home," double-time.

She advances as he plays, stops three yards away.

MILO

A motorcycle and a harp—what else? What you bring Rosacoke? What you bring me?

WESLEY

(Bowing at the waist, hand on his heart; rising with a smile for Rosa) My actual self. No— *(To Milo, shaking his harmonica)* I took a few lessons on this from a friend.

MILO

I'm sure you took all grades of lessons, day-school and night-school. Just don't be teaching my sister your lessons. See what I mean?—I been teaching Sissie. *(Pats Sissie's belly)* Ain't she a good learner? *(Mock-whisper to Sissie)* At least it hasn't gone to your head, Doll-baby.

SISSIE

Milo, I said I was sick as a dog. Let's roll this car to that damned picnic and find some shade.

MILO

Calm down, Sugar. Take a lesson from Rosa. She turned a new leaf time she heard that cycle.

EMMA

Sissie's right—we've got to get started. Wesley, are you coming to the picnic with us?

WESLEY

If you've got plenty food.

MILO

We could feed the five thousand. But how about you taking Rosa to the funeral? Then you two come on to the picnic together.

WESLEY

I'm not dressed.

MILO

It's a nigger funeral.

EMMA

Milo, Rosa's not well. She can't go bumping through the dust today.

MILO

Of course she can—can't you, Rosa? Sure thing. Put your hat in the saddlebags and, Wesley, go slow. Be a lovely ride. Rosa's first time. First time for everything, Rosa. Come on!

Rosa takes off her hat and moves toward Milo.

He snatches at Wesley, pulls his sailor cap off, jams it down on Rosa's head.

MILO

She's in service now!

Rosa accepts it all, having reached Wesley, though they haven't touched.

EMMA

Go easy, Milo. Everybody's not brass.

MILO

Not only going easy—I'm spreading joy.

Rosa moves to leave.

Wesley watches a moment, then follows her off.

MILO

See you at the lake. *(Cycle fires, starts)* You got to pull your dress up!

No one waves

The cycle leaves.

Emma watches after everyone else has moved toward the car.

2

An hour later, Mount Moriah Church, a coffin on trestles, piano music.

Mrs. Ransom stands.

MRS. RANSOM

It is now my duty to read the obituary over this child we all knew and cherished. Miss Mildred Sutton was born in 1936 in the bed where she died. Her mother is Mary Sutton of this community; and her father was Wallace Sutton, now gone. She grew up round here and worked in tobacco for Mr. Isaac Alston and went to school till she started cooking for the Drakes and tending their children that she loved like they were hers. They are at the beach now or would surely be here. Mildred hoped to go with them right to the last and then wasn't able. She stayed here and died on her twenty-first birthday. Her favorite song was "Annie Laurie," which she learned from Miss Rosacoke Mustian who is with us today, representing Mildred's many white friends; and I welcome her here on behalf of the family in their hour of need. I will sing the song now to remember Mildred. *(Lifts her head and begins, no accompaniment)*

"Maxwellton's braes are bonnie where early falls the dew;
And 'twas there that Annie Laurie gave me her promise true,
Gave me her promise true which ne'er forgot would be;
And for bonnie Annie Laurie I'd lay me doun and dee."

Mrs. Ransom sits.

Sammy Ransom and Rev. Mingie rise, lift the coffin lid.

REV. MINGIE

Miss Rosacoke, please view Mildred now.

ROSACOKE

Now?

REV. MINGIE

She's ready now.

Piano starts softly.

Rosa stands, comes forward slowly, looks down at the body.

MARY

Testify. Testify for Mildred, Rosacoke.

Voices say "Yes—testify—Amen." Soft music continues. Wesley's cycle fires and starts, though it doesn't move.

ROSACOKE

I hadn't seen much of Mildred lately, but we always observed each other's birthday; and the other evening I said to myself "It's Mildred's twenty-first birthday; I should find her," so I walked down to her place after supper and nobody was there but the turkey— *(A child's high voice laughs two notes; the cycle roars, then idles. Rosa offers the rest to Mary)* See, I didn't know till the next afternoon you had carried her off. There I was just wanting to give her a pair of stockings and wish her a long and happy life, and she was already gone.

The cycle leaves—slowly through the churchyard, pauses, swells, then rapidly fades.

Rosa shakes her head to Mary, stands another moment, half-runs out.

MARY

Sammy, go help her.

Sammy Ransom rises from beside Mr. Isaac Alston and follows Rosa out.

She stands in the churchyard, staring at the road.

Sammy stops on the top step.

Rosa hears him and turns.

ROSACOKE

Aren't you frying in all that wool?

SAMMY

I'm all right. What's wrong, Rosacoke?

ROSACOKE

(Pauses, then knows) Everybody I know is gone. *(Tears come silently)*

SAMMY

I'm here; you know me. And if you're needing to go somewhere, Sammy can take you.

ROSACOKE

Place I need to go is too long a ride for you and Mr. Isaac.

SAMMY

Where's that?

ROSACOKE

The laughing academy. No, thank you, Sammy, but I'm going home and I can walk that.

SAMMY

In this heat today?

ROSACOKE

We've played baseball in worse than this—you and me and Mildred. Sammy, go back. I've ruined things enough without taking you away. Tell Mary I'm sorry.

SAMMY

No telling where Wesley is, Rosacoke, with that machine.

ROSACOKE

No, maybe not but you know I've got to find him.

SAMMY

Good luck then.

ROSACOKE

Same to you. We need it.

She leaves.

Sammy watches her out of sight.

3

A half-hour later, a clearing in Mr. Isaac's woods.

Rosa enters, moves toward a spring, kicks off her shoes, tests the water with a foot.

ROSACOKE

Alaska! *(Sinks both feet in)* If any of you snakes are still in there, you can have these feet and welcome to them! *(Sits awhile, eyes shut, head back, hat beside her. Then she looks down, draws her dress high on her thighs and rubs their smoothness)* White as a fish belly. Never mind. You're saving it, Honey, till the right time comes. Whenever that is, whenever that is.

Wesley enters behind her, comes silently forward; and stands behind her, staring down.

ROSACOKE

What do you know about this spring?

WESLEY

I know somebody has stirred hell out of it.

ROSACOKE

That was Rosacoke. Remember her? She was rinsing her feet; they were badly in need. *(Lowers her dress, takes her hat and stands)* I don't stir springs up every day, Wesley. I don't strike out for home in the blistering dust every day either; try to plan my life a little better than that.

WESLEY

Ought not to have planned on Wesley then.

ROSACOKE

That may well be.

WESLEY

You ready for this picnic?

ROSACOKE

I'm forgetting that. By the time we got there, they'd all be gone—

WESLEY

Who are they, Rosa? I didn't know we were going to see them.

ROSACOKE

—And you haven't said a word about where you went in the midst of Mildred's funeral, making me look like a barefaced fool.

WESLEY

I went to get something I hope to need, and I never asked you to act like a fool.

ROSACOKE

I can't go looking like the Tarbaby. You'll have to stop at home and let me change.

WESLEY

Clothes aren't what you need. Everybody'll look like Tarbabies by now, hot as it is.

ROSACOKE

I'm not everybody.

WESLEY

I knew that. *(Smiles, extends a hand to her)*

ROSACOKE

(Holds her separate ground) Then tell me who you are.

WESLEY

The one standing here. The one that's here to see you. *(Extends the hand again)*

ROSACOKE

How did you find me?

WESLEY

You found me, remember? I was up a tree, peaceful.

ROSACOKE

No, here—now, I mean.

WESLEY

(Shuts his eyes, draws breath through his nose) I could find you on the moon.

ROSACOKE

Don't strain your powers. This is North Carolina.

WESLEY

All one place to me—you're in it; I found you.

Rosa takes his hand finally; they leave together.

4

Mid-afternoon, Mason's Lake, Virginia; Delight Church picnic. Emma and Sissie sit in the shade, Marise and Macey Gupton nearby.

Milo and Willie Duke Aycock scramble at water's edge.

WILLIE

Milo, stop! You're a married man.

Wesley and Rosa enter and watch.

MILO

Damn right, I'm married—and love every minute—but you ain't, Honey; and you ain't getting Wesley. He belongs to the Mustians.

EMMA AND SISSIE

Milo!

Willie has struggled free and moves toward the women's bath-house.

MILO

Willie, I warned you. Rosa, hold him down—the enemy's approaching.

WILLIE

Hey, Wesley. Hey, Rosa.

ROSACOKE

Hey, Willie.

MILO

(Rearranging his crotch) Come on in, Wesley, but stay off that slide. I've ruined myself—don't deprive Rosa of a lovely future.

ROSACOKE

Milo, behave. This is Sunday, remember?

BABY SISTER

(Runs in) You missed the baptizing. I've baptized all the Guptons today, some more than once.

WESLEY

Glad you got them before they passed on.

BABY SISTER

You two don't look so good yourselves.

ROSACOKE

Where's Mama?

BABY SISTER

Nursing Sissie yonder in the shade.

Wesley moves toward the bathhouse; Rosa toward her mother, skirting the lake, taking her time.

MILO

(From the lake) Come on, Rosa. Stand up for your rights!

Rosa ignores him but quickens her step toward Emma, still fanning a prostrate Sissie.

EMMA

Fix your hair, Rosa. You look like you rode in on a circular saw.

ROSACOKE

If that's what you call a motorcycle, I did.

SISSIE

I wish somebody had took me riding on a motorcycle on a rocky road five months ago, and I wouldn't be sick as a dog today.

ROSACOKE

What's wrong with Sissie?

EMMA

Nothing. How was the funeral?

ROSACOKE

Mama, it wasn't a show.

EMMA

I know that. I just thought you might have heard who was father to Mildred's baby.

SISSIE

I'll tell you who the father of this baby is— *(Hits her belly a thud)*

Wesley runs from the bathhouse, calls "Milo" and dives.

SISSIE

—That fool by the slide acting five years old. And if I have anything tamer than a monkey, I'll be a lot luckier than your black friend Mildred.

But Rosa watches Wesley.

EMMA

He can dive all right—Wesley. Can't he?

ROSACOKE

He can do that.

EMMA

They must be trying to touch the bottom. It's twenty-feet deep.

SISSIE

If they're on the bottom, they're eat-up with leeches.

EMMA

Wesley's too speedy for any leech to catch.

ROSACOKE

Amen.

SISSIE

Well, I can't speak for the leeches of course; but Willie Duke Aycock has taken hold.

EMMA

Willie can't keep up with those boys long, can't swim good as a window weight.

SISSIE

No, but she can float—got God's own waterwings in her halter. Remember her winning that Dairy Princess contest?—nearly broke up school for a month: boys laughing.

ROSACOKE

I don't notice Milo swimming away from her.

SISSIE

Milo can swim her to Mesopotamia, but he's on a rope and the end of that rope is anchored right here. *(Pats her belly, smiles)*

EMMA

(To Rosa) Consider the source.

ROSACOKE

Yes ma'm, I'll try.

Rosa wanders off, still watching the lake; approaches the Guptons—Marise sitting, Macey and Frederick asleep.

MARISE

Don't step on my baby, Rosacoke.

ROSACOKE

I'm sorry. I was watching the swimming, Marise. You been swimming?

The baby—Frederick—launches a yell.

MARISE

Haven't swam since before my first baby. *(Wraps Frederick tighter in his blanket; his crying grows frantic)*

ROSACOKE

He's roasting.

MARISE

No, he's not. *(Opens her dress, lifts Frederick to her breast, gently chides him)* Just wait for once.

Milo and Wesley enter with a kicking Willie in their arms, dump her like a sack.

WILLIE

(To Wesley) Child, you have grown.

MILO

Drown, Willie. Go on and drown. No demand for you.

Willie stands, abandoned, and enters the bathhouse.

MACEY

(Wakened by the skirmish) Milo's doing his duty for you, Rosa.

ROSACOKE

(Smiles, embarrassed; looks down to Marise) Marise, I'll see you—

Marise is lost in her suckling baby; Rosa moves again to her mother.

Milo spots her, runs, picks her up, delivers her at Emma's feet.

Rosa fumbles to a dignified posture. Milo rummages in Sissie's bag, finds two cigars, lights both at once.

Wesley approaches.

EMMA

Milo, I asked you once to go easy. Everybody's not as strong as you.

MILO

(Lays a gentle hand on Rosa's leg) I don't mean harm.

ROSACOKE

I'll remember that.

EMMA

That leech means harm. *(Points to Wesley's leg)*

A leech is fastened to Wesley's thigh. He picks at it, halts in repulsion, stamps his foot.

Rosa comes forward on her knees, looks, touches it.

EMMA

Don't pull it off; he'll bleed to death.

MILO

Leave it alone. It's hungry like me and Wesley won't miss that little drop of blood. Do you good. Cool you down. Ease your pressure.

WESLEY

I can ease my pressure other ways, Milo, than by things on me; and if you're so interested in feeding dumb animals, I'll stick him on you soon as I get him off.

MILO

Take your cigar and burn him off—a gift to celebrate my baby boy.

SISSIE

(To Milo) Count your chickens when they chirp.

Wesley takes the cigar, tries to touch the leech but slips and burns his thigh. He holds it out to Rosa.

WESLEY

Do it please.

Rosa takes the cigar, flicks the ash off neatly and accurately touches the leech's mouth. It flaps to the ground; she stamps it with her shoe, held in her hand; then she ties Wesley's wound with a long white handkerchief from her pocket.

MILO

Thank her, Son. She saved your life.

WESLEY

She knows I thank her.

MILO

Saying is believing.

WESLEY

Thank you.

ROSACOKE

You're welcome.

They take a silent moment to calm themselves—both the men lying (Wesley on his stomach), Sissie propped in her daze, Rosa reclining on one elbow, only Emma sitting up.

Baby Sister wanders up from the lake, also calmed by fatigue.

BABY SISTER

Mr. Isaac's come.

Sammy Ransom enters with Mr. Isaac's armchair, places it, leaves, returns with Mr. Isaac in his arms, seats him carefully.

ROSACOKE

Wonder why he came this far in the sun to sit a few minutes in that old chair?

MILO

Probably planning to buy the lake—owns everybody in it.

ROSACOKE

Milo, feed your face and hush. Some people in the world think of something but money even if you can't.

MILO

I'll think of anything you name, Red Rose, if you'll make Mr. Isaac pay me all he owes this family—Granddaddy, Daddy, me:

fifty years of chewing dust in his hard fields so he can pay a trained ape to haul him round.

ROSACOKE

He went to Mildred's funeral, which few here did.

MILO

Didn't have a choice there—didn't Sammy have to go?

ROSACOKE

Meaning what?

MILO

Meaning that is the nigger killed your friend Mildred by stuffing her guts with a bastard boy and not seeing to her when her time came.

ROSACOKE

You can't prove that.

MILO

No, and Mildred couldn't either. If you back up into an airplane motor, you can't name the one blade slices you first.

EMMA

That's enough, Milo. Joke but don't lie. Mr. Isaac isn't looking for money and you know it. He's living out the end of the life he was handed; you'll have to do the same. You want him to die just because you're young? We've worked for him, sure—it was work or eat gravel—but he's been good to us. The night that truck killed your drunk father, I was sitting in the back room, blind with grief, wondering could I ever feed four helpless children, when I heard a knock and went to the door. There was Mr. Isaac handing me fifty dollars, folded small as my thumbnail, saying "Emma, I guess he is far better off."

MILO

Fifty dollars—ummm. *(Kisses air loudly)* Thank you, Mr. Isaac. You saved four lives. Milo worked all those years just because he loved it. Any rest would have ruined him.

Emma gathers to answer but Baby Sister sings.

BABY SISTER

"Praise God from whom all blessings flow.
Praise Him all creatures here below.
Praise Him above ye heavenly host.
Praise Father, Son, and Holy Ghost."

On "Ghost," Frederick Gupton cries again.

EMMA

You scared him, Sister, mentioning ghosts.

MILO

All that baby needs is a bust in the mouth.

WESLEY

(Pushing up with sudden boldness) —What they all need.

EMMA

Hush.

SISSIE

He's had it twice already since noon.

MILO

Nobody ever gets enough—do they, Wesley? *(Searches a box, finds a chicken leg, eats it)*

Wesley doesn't answer but Macey Gupton rises and comes to Milo.

MACEY

You people staying on for supper, Milo?

MILO

Yeah, spending the weekend—camping out.

Macey accepts the rebuff with a smile, waves, heads back to Marise.

EMMA

Don't tell a lie.

MILO

You know he was fishing for an invitation to bring that squad of peeled squirrels over here and eat our stuff.

EMMA

They could have what Rosa and Wesley haven't touched—you children eat something.

Rosa shakes her head No.

WESLEY

I'm fine, Mrs. Mustian.

EMMA

You'll both die by dark.

MILO

Leave them be. They got private means of nourishment.

Since Milo's rebuff, the Guptons have slowly prepared to leave.

Rosa has watched with willful attention. Wesley secretly works a hand to her leg.

WESLEY

Look at me.

ROSACOKE

I'm watching God's beautiful sunset, Wesley—beats any human sight at hand.

WESLEY

Not me. Not you. I've come a long way to see one human. *(Presses her leg again. She will not respond)*

ROSACOKE

Sit still then and look. Stop running and watch.

WESLEY

I was watching when you found me, the first day ever.

ROSACOKE

Not me though, Wesley. You barely saw me.

WESLEY

That's your one opinion. There's at least one more. I've come here today. I'm watching just you.

ROSACOKE

Put your shades on then.

Wesley laughs gently, watches.

Willie emerges dressed from the bathhouse, looks toward Wesley.

MACEY

Willie, we're ready.

WILLIE

One minute, Macey.

Willie moves toward Wesley.

Baby Sister moans.

Milo grins toward Rosa, about to speak.

EMMA

Milo, pass me that basket and don't say a word.

Milo obeys.

All watch Willie pass.

WILLIE

How're you, Mrs. Mustian? Wesley, can I speak to you?

Wesley waits a moment, then flings himself up and follows Willie four steps from Rosa.

Willie whispers to him; he smiles and shrugs—neither Yes nor No.

WILLIE

O.K. I'll wait. *(Heads toward the Guptons, who straggle away)*

Wesley slowly moves back to Rosa, sits—not lies—in his previous place. Embarrassed moments.

MILO

How many more?

WESLEY

More what?

MILO

Women trailing you. Bet they're strung up the road clear from here to Norfolk, waiting on you to pass.

No answer from Wesley.

SISSIE

Milo just wishes he had a few, Wesley.

MILO

How you know I don't have a stable full?

SISSIE

If you do, Sissie's got the key to your stable, Son.

EMMA

You all ought to kneel in the dirt right here and thank God above He doesn't strike you dumb.

MILO

I'm joking, Mama—a little vacation. No need to tune in.

EMMA

I wasn't tuned in. I was thinking how lucky every one of you is—resting and fed. Think of your brother and what he's doing.

MILO

Rato is happy as a coot where he is—all he can eat of that good Army food, making twice as much money as he'd ever make here with the brain he got.

EMMA

I wasn't worried about him eating, and he got all the brain the Lord intended. I was just regretting he missed Mildred's funeral—off in flat Oklahoma, marching for the government on a Sunday hot as this.

ROSACOKE

(With sudden bitterness) Why didn't you go then and write him a description?

EMMA

My duty was with my own.

ROSACOKE

Deviling eggs for Milo to choke on?—that what you call your own? And fanning the flies off Sissie's belly? And keeping Baby Sister from drowning the Guptons? I'm glad you're so sure of what's yours and what's not.

EMMA

I don't see why you're acting so grand. You said yourself you didn't stay to the end.

ROSACOKE

No, I didn't. You want to know why? Because Wesley Beavers wouldn't sit with me in respect to the dead but stayed in the churchyard, shining that engine; and then when they called me to witness for Mildred, he cranked up and tore off and left me and I ran.

MILO

You can't get upset every time Wesley leaves. All us tomcats got to make our rounds.

ROSACOKE

Milo, you've turned out to be one of the sorriest people I know.

MILO

Thank you, ma'm. What about your friend Wesley here?

Rosa looks to Wesley—the back of his head; he does not turn.

ROSACOKE

I don't know about my friend Wesley. I don't know what he plans one minute to the next. I don't know my place in that line of women you say is strung waiting from here to Norfolk.

MILO

Wesley, what is Rosa's place in your string of ladies? Being her oldest brother, it's my duty to ask.

Wesley lies still a moment, then suddenly rolls and faces Rosa—staring at her chest as if searching for a number, her place in line. When he opens his mouth to speak, she runs barefoot to the edge of the lake.

EMMA

What have you done to Rosacoke, Wesley?

WESLEY

Not a thing, Mrs. Mustian. I hadn't said a word.

EMMA

Try saying some then. She's sick on silence.

MILO

It's her battery, Wesley—battery needs charging. You know how to charge up a battery, don't you?

EMMA

The child's had a sadder day than any of you know.

MILO

Sad over what?

EMMA

Mildred's funeral, all *this*—

MILO

No use grieving about that funeral. I knew Mildred as long as Rosa, and Mildred didn't get a thing she didn't ask for—giving herself to any boy that passed. Nothing happens to people that they don't ask for.

EMMA

(Struggles to her feet, takes the box of supper from Milo's lap) I'm asking you to take me home. That's the sorriest thing you've said in years, and the sun is going down. Mildred Sutton was twenty-one years old and—black, blue, or green—she died in

pain. Baby Sister, come help me fold this blanket. *(Sissie, Milo and Wesley stand ashamed as Emma and Baby Sister prepare to leave. Ready, Emma moves to Wesley; speaks privately)* Wesley, do you think you can ease that child?

WESLEY

I'll try.

EMMA

And bring her home safe and not abuse her feelings?

WESLEY

Mrs. Mustian, other people have feelings real as hers, which they can't speak.

EMMA

She's forcing us to break her.

WESLEY

I don't want that.

EMMA

She's chosen you for it. Leave her to me, Wesley—here now, clean—or learn how to bear her.

They both wait, looking at Rosa's back.

Wesley turns to Emma.

WESLEY

I'm still here, you notice.

EMMA

Can I hold you to that?

WESLEY

If I get any help.

Emma nods again, turns.

Milo, Sissie and Baby Sister straggle off.

Emma stops at Mr. Isaac's chair.

EMMA

Mr. Isaac, you staying till they drain the lake?

MR. ISAAC

I'm staying till last. I like to be last.

EMMA

Well, you're doing fine at it. You can go now though. Those children don't know you're left in the world. He'll be getting tired, Sammy.

SAMMY

He'll tell me, Mrs. Mustian.

Emma touches Mr. Isaac on the shoulder and leaves.

As the following starts, Mr. Isaac signs to Sammy, who walks him off; then returns for the chair.

Wesley moves toward Rosa slowly in silence, sits behind her, lays one hand across her eyes.

WESLEY

Who am I?

ROSACOKE

(At once) You're Wesley. *(Waits)* That doesn't say why you act the way you do.

WESLEY

Because I'm Wesley. You asked to know Wesley.

ROSACOKE

(Thinks, nods) Here comes a breeze.

They savor it a moment; then Wesley lays a hand on Rosa's knee.

WESLEY

Let's swim before it's night.

ROSACOKE

What would I swim in?—my lily-white skin? This filthy dress is all I've got.

WESLEY

You could rent one over at the drink stand there.

ROSACOKE

I wouldn't put on a public bathing suit if I never touched water, and I thought you got a bellyful of underwater sports with Willie Duke Aycock.

WESLEY

No.

ROSACOKE

No what?

WESLEY

No, I didn't get a bellyful.

He smiles but she pulls away, repelled again. He sees his error, hopes to mend it, stands, leaves. The sounds of his diving begin.

Rosa watches.

Mr. Mason approaches behind, watches too.

MR. MASON

Young lady, what kin is that boy to you?

ROSACOKE

No kin. I came with him. We're the scraps of Delight Church picnic is all. He just got out of the Navy—that boy—and he's trying to recall every trick he learned.

MR. MASON

He must be, yes. I wish he wasn't doing it on my time though. I mean I'm a preacher, and I got to go preach, and the law says nobody dives when I ain't watching. He can swim great rings round me, I know; but Delight Church paid me to lifeguard you—so long as he dives, I got to guard.

ROSACOKE

Wesley, Mr. Mason has got to go home.

WESLEY

(At a distance) Go easy, Mr. Mason.

MR. MASON

(Waves, laughs) Lady, I'm going to leave him alone and deputize you a lifeguard for him. You look strong enough. He's your life to save from here on in. *(Takes out his watch)* It's six-thirty now and I'm preaching in an hour. What must I preach on, Lady?

ROSACOKE

If you don't know by now, I'm glad I haven't got to listen. *(Smiles)*

MR. MASON

What I mean to say is, give me your favorite text; and that's what I'll preach on.

ROSACOKE

(Thinks briefly) "Then Jesus asked him what is thy name and he said Legion."

MR. MASON

(Lost, then at last) Yes ma'm, that is a humdinger. *(Pauses)* Hope you people enjoyed your day. Come back to see me anytime it's hot. I'm always here; so's the water. *(Goes four steps; turns again to see Wesley, then Rosa; speaks with genuine concern)* Take care of him, Lady. He's younger than I thought.

ROSACOKE

Twenty-two years old—been to Spain and France.

MR. MASON

Twenty-two's barely strong enough to walk. Jesus never spoke a sound till he was past thirty.

ROSACOKE

He thought a lot though.

MR. MASON

(Thinks again, smiles) You win them all, don't you? Got a fine gift, Lady—confound babes and fools. Just use it right please.

Rosa nods; he leaves.

She turns back toward Wesley.

WESLEY

(Still distant) Rosa, you got anything I can drink?

ROSACOKE

What you mean?

WESLEY

I mean I'm thirsty.

ROSACOKE

You're standing in several thousand tons of spring water. *(Goes on watching as Wesley approaches, soaked and serious)* The drink stand is closed. We're on our own.

Wesley nods, extends a hand to her hair, stops short of a touch, moves off to the bathhouse.

Rosa thinks they are leaving, goes to find her shoes and hat. She puts on her shoes as Wesley appears in the bathhouse door, having added only a shirt to his trunks.

ROSACOKE

Who stole your pants?

WESLEY

Rosa, come here.

Wesley waves her to him.

She goes, takes his proffered hand; and he leads them off on a walk round the lake. After six slow steps and silence from Wesley, Rosa stops.

ROSACOKE

Aren't we going home? Mr. Mason has shut it; maybe we should go.

WESLEY

Maybe I can find some drinking water.

ROSACOKE

(Accepting his lead again but with protest) Wesley, there is water at every gas station between here and home. Why have we got to go tearing through some strange somebody's bushes?

WESLEY

(Stops) Please hush, Rosa. *(Strokes her hair)*

ROSACOKE

(Steps away, touches her hair quickly) Sun has bleached me till I look like a tramp.

WESLEY

What would you know about a tramp, bleached or black?

ROSACOKE

I know you don't have to go to Norfolk to find one.

WESLEY

What do you mean?

ROSACOKE

You know who I mean.

WESLEY

If it's Willie you mean, she'll be in Norfolk tomorrow morning with all the other tramps you know.

ROSACOKE

What's she going for?

WESLEY

To ease her pain. *(Smiles)* No, she's got a job.

ROSACOKE

Doing what?

WESLEY

Curling hair.

ROSACOKE

What does she know about curling hair with that mess she's got?

WESLEY

I don't know but she's moving up, bag and baggage.

ROSACOKE

What was she asking you about then?

WESLEY

Would I ride her up.

ROSACOKE

On that motorcycle?—a hundred-thirty miles?

WESLEY

Yes.

ROSACOKE

Then she's crazier than even I thought she was. *(Moves two steps away)* Are you taking her?

WESLEY

Don't know yet.

ROSACOKE

When will you know?

WESLEY

Time I'm home tonight.

Wesley goes to her, takes her hand again; they walk on farther to trees above the lake.

Rosa finally pulls at his lead.

ROSACOKE

We'll both catch terrible poison-oak—which Milo will laugh at till Christmas at least—and you won't find any water up here.

WESLEY

Maybe water's not what I'm looking for.

ROSACOKE

I don't notice gold dust lying around—what are you hunting?

Wesley leads her to a large tree and sits beneath it.

Rosa holds his hand but doesn't sit.

ROSACOKE

Night'll come and catch us here, and we'll get scratched to pieces stumbling out.

Wesley looks up, not smiling; pulls her hand.

She sits beside him and smooths her hair.

He takes her smoothing hand, lifts her hair and kisses her neck.

She sits upright, eyes open, face clenching.

Wesley works on till she pulls away.

ROSACOKE

How much else did you learn in the Navy?—harmonica playing, motorcycle riding, gnawing on girls like sides of meat. Uncle Sam got his money's worth in you. *(Wesley sits far back, his face all dark)* Wesley, where are you?

WESLEY

I was right there with you. *(Waits)* I'm here, I guess.

ROSACOKE

You guess. You *guess?* Do you guess I'm made out of brass like Willie to trail behind you and beg for notice? You guess I can sit on another seven years, wondering who Wesley is and where Wesley is and is Wesley ever coming home, calming down, resting long enough to have him a life? You guess I can live on in mystery like this till you finally decide to come out of cover and speak your mind?—say "Rosa, I'm ready to carry my share" or "Rosa, get your fool self home to your Mama." All I'm asking you to do is say. Do you guess you love me or that I love you?

WESLEY

(Waits, still dark; then his voice half-strange) I've answered that the only way I know how. I'm here by you. *(Moves forward far enough to take light again)*

ROSACOKE

(Studies him closely) I love you, Wesley. When I see you, I do. I

know this isn't what a girl ought to say; but when you have sat silent seven whole years, waiting for somebody you love to speak and you don't know one reason why you love them or even what you want them to say—then there comes a time when you have to speak. I've spoken and I'm here.

WESLEY

I knew that, Rosa. Wesley is here.

He begins his answer the way he can—gently kissing her eyes, lips, neck; then moving downward.

At first she responds, then balks and stops him with her hand.

ROSACOKE

Is that everything you want out of me?

WESLEY

It's right much, Rosa. *(Waits)* We're not exactly strangers. Listen, if you're thinking of Mildred's trouble, you'll be all right. It's why I left the funeral— *(Touches his shirt pocket)*

ROSACOKE

(Stands suddenly) Take me home please. It's nearly night.

WESLEY

Of course it's night. What the hell you want—floodlights?

ROSACOKE

I said take me home.

WESLEY

You say a lot, Rosa—more than you understand. Try living those words. *(She does not turn so Wesley stands)* You know I'm going to Norfolk tomorrow. You know that, don't you?

ROSACOKE

I know it. *(Moves to leave)*

WESLEY

And that maybe I'm riding Willie up there?

ROSACOKE

You can ride Willie up the seaboard coast, if she's what you want. Just take care she doesn't have Mildred's trouble either.

Rosa leaves and waits near the bathhouse—full night now.

Wesley follows separately, slowly; enters the bathhouse, comes out with his clothes. Facing Rosa, three steps away, he slides off his trunks; stands bare before her—to punish and tempt her. Then slowly, still watching her, he dresses.

She bears the sight with no visible response.

WESLEY

You ever know that you really want me—not a dream about me but a person you can see and touch: *not you*—you let me know.

Rosa nods, moves quickly off.

Wesley follows slowly.

ACT TWO

1

The Mustian house, a Saturday afternoon in early November.

Baby Sister sits on the porch in a sweater.

Rosa enters in a dark winter coat, turns and waves behind to her unseen driver.

ROSACOKE

Thank you, Mr. Coleman. I'll see you Monday morning.

His car drives off.

BABY SISTER

Hear anything good today?

ROSACOKE

(Moves slowly up, sits on the steps, thinks, then smiles) How about this? —I was putting through a call from some man in Vaughan to a woman in Weldon. The first word he said was "Precious, it's *over.*"

BABY SISTER

What did she say?

ROSACOKE

She waited a minute—I thought I'd broke the circuit—and then in a voice that would saw baked bricks, she said "Little Buddy, that's what *you* think. I air-conditioned my car for you, and I'm not lying in it out here by myself!"

BABY SISTER

What else?

ROSACOKE

She hung up. Otherwise, the usual funerals and wrecks. I'm worn flat out from other people's news. *(She sits on a moment, eyes shut, leaning back; then stands to go in—tired but not unhappy. She has touched the door before Baby Sister speaks)*

BABY SISTER

You can stop waiting now.

ROSACOKE

Was I waiting?

BABY SISTER

Yes.

ROSACOKE

(Lightly) For Jesus to call me to heaven and rest. For my hair to curl by itself in the night—

BABY SISTER

For a letter. You got it. I put it on your mantel.

Rosa opens the door and enters, not running but intent as she climbs to her room.

Baby Sister calls behind her.

BABY SISTER

You're supposed to say thank you.

ROSACOKE

Thank you.

As Rosa climbs, her room is lighted.

Sissie is there at the window with the letter, straining to read it through the envelope. She is nine months pregnant.

Rosa finds her there.

ROSACOKE

Leave!

SISSIE

I was dusting your things, trying to help.

ROSACOKE

Get out, Sissie.

SISSIE

It's all the doctor will let me do—a little dusting.

ROSACOKE

(Snatches her letter) And a little reading? Don't strain your eyes.

SISSIE

Thank you, Miss God-in-Heaven, I won't. *(Moves toward the door, turns)* And neither will you, not reading that—gone more than three months and writes two lines.

ROSACOKE

Sissie Abbott, just don't forget who you are and how you are in this house of ours—catching Milo like you did.

SISSIE

(Limps out the door, holding chest and belly) Milo, help me!

The following is clearly heard from the stairs while Rosa shuts and locks her door, wipes the letter on her coat and opens it.

MILO

Has your time come, Sugar?

SISSIE

I don't know, Milo, and I don't care. I'd be better dead than bringing children to this house.

MILO

What's wrong now?

SISSIE

I was dusting Rosa's room when she ran in just now and yelled things to me I wouldn't whisper to a dog.

MILO

Like what?

SISSIE

She said I had no right to be here, that I got you dishonest—

MILO

(Running to Rosa's door and knocking) Rosa, who the hell do you think you are, abusing Sissie when she's ten days overdue? You trying to kill her? *(Waits for word; there is none)* Speak to me—I feed your face.

ROSACOKE

(Moves to the door but leaves it shut) You don't. I work as hard as you.

MILO

I'll trade you then. *(Rosa opens quickly and faces him gravely)* —You run this farm from now till next fall, and I'll make long-distance calls for rich folks and snoop in on them.

ROSACOKE

(Thinks, nods, extends the letter) A deal—start now. Start by answering this. Everybody else here has read it. Go on.

MILO

I'll start Monday morning. You keep your own mail. I'm already married.

SISSIE

(Unseen) Milo, please.

MILO

(Calls toward her gently) Just get calm now. If the baby's coming, I'll call Dr. Sledge. If he's not, just rest. Rest's what we all need.

ROSACOKE

Amen to that.

Milo gives a little half-apologetic wave and goes downstairs.

Rosa shuts her door, moves again to her window.

Emma meets Milo at the foot of the stairs.

EMMA

Has Sissie started?

MILO

I doubt it. She was helping out, dusting Rosa's room. Rosa walked in while Sissie was touching a letter from Wesley—nothing to it.

Emma nods and at once a great roar starts above.

MILO

What the hell is that?

EMMA

An airplane—

They both run to the porch.

MILO

Crashing—or landing hard.

EMMA

In Aycock's field.

SISSIE

(Inside) Mi-lo—

MILO

Sugar, hold on. Mama, go sit with Sissie. I better go see how many dead fools we got.

Milo goes.

Emma climbs a few steps, listens.

EMMA

Sissie, you all right?

SISSIE

(Unseen) I can't say now.

EMMA

Then I'll ask you later. *(Waits, looks upward, then climbs to Rosa and opens the door)*

ROSACOKE

(From her bed, half-risen) Mama, I've begged everybody to knock.

EMMA

Don't make me mad before I can speak. I've climbed fourteen high steps to talk to you.

ROSACOKE

What about?

EMMA

I wanted to show you this old picture I found today. *(Reaches to her pocket for a stiff tan photograph, offers it to Rosa)*

ROSACOKE

(Still reclining, takes the picture) Who is it of?

EMMA

I can't place the stout one; the tall one is your father.

ROSACOKE

(Rises slowly, turns it over) "Ocean View, Virginia. July 1915." *(Waits, faces Emma)* I never saw him so clear before.

EMMA

I never knew there was his likeness in the world, except what Milo has got round his eyes; and then I found this old box of collars. It must have been the time your grandfather took them to water for the day. It amounted to the only trip he ever gave them, and it ended awful because he put a five-dollar bill in his shoe in case of emergency and then walked ten miles up and down the sand. About leaving time, emergencies arose—one was your father wanting a plaster-Paris statue of Mutt and Jeff—so your grandfather sat down and took his shoe off; and the money was just little soggy crumbs. He'd worn it out. He talked about that for thirty years.

ROSACOKE

(Still studying the picture) Had you seen him by then?

EMMA

Many times.

ROSACOKE

Did you know him?

EMMA

Good as I ever did. I don't mean to say we passed time together—we were nothing but babies—but I used to see him sometime at church, and at Sunday-school picnics he generally wound up eating with us—my mother had the freest hand on earth; the Mustians were *close.* So I mostly saw him eating Mama's pie or cake—he was crazy for sweets. *(Reaches for the picture, studies it; continues half-privately, almost to herself)* Funny thing is, this is how I see him, whenever I see him—looking like this, so young and serious, not like he got to be. *(Stands with the picture and walks to Rosa's window, continues quietly but to Rosa again)* If he would have stayed this way, Rosacoke, he'd be here this minute, helping us all. But he started to change. People have to change—I well know that—but he didn't have a dead leaf's will-power; so time did the changing on him, every step: and every step was down. He didn't have a thing he controlled but his looks—and you can't spend looks, can't feed them to children, can't go on begging people's pardon for hurts just because you look the way he did then. Still I never asked for anything else—not in 1930. Then when money got scarce as hen's back teeth, and his drunks commenced coming so close together they were one long drunk, and he was sleeping nights wherever he dropped in fields or by the road—I took it all like a bluefaced fool: it was take it or jump down the well and die. I never asked him to change a thing till it was too late, and he had filled me up with four big babies and himself to the eyes with bootleg liquor and then walked into a pickup truck going fifty miles an hour like it was a bed. But like I say, I don't recall him that way and I'm thankful. *(Rubs the picture on her apron to dust it; then walks to the mantel, props it there by one of Wesley)* I'll leave it here so you can see it—be yours someday anyhow. None of the others would want it. *(Turns, studies Rosa)* Rosa, I've pressed some old baby clothes. Get up and take them to Mildred's baby please.

ROSACOKE

Mama, let me rest.

EMMA

Rest isn't what you need. You need to get up and live your life among people that love you—that have proved they love you for long years, Rosa. *(No reply from Rosa, reclining again)* Did the letter upset you?

ROSACOKE

No.

EMMA

How is he doing?

ROSACOKE

He never says that.

EMMA

What does he say?

ROSACOKE

(Waits) That he might come down some weekend soon if I make up my mind to tell him to and meet him halfway.

EMMA

Where would that be?—Courtland?

ROSACOKE

You know where it would be.

EMMA

Then tell him to step in the ocean and cool. And you stop waiting.

ROSACOKE

He isn't what I'm waiting for.

EMMA

Don't lie to me. What else is there but Judgment Day?

ROSACOKE

My whole life ahead. I mean to have a life.

EMMA

Then get up and start it—

Rosa half-sits, mouth working silently.

Milo runs in—porch, stairs—throws open Rosa's door.

MILO

Cares are ended!

EMMA

Milo, go easy. Sissie's expecting.

MILO

So am I, Mama. Rosa, that little airplane landed on purpose. Guess who was in it? *(Rushes to answer himself)* —Willie Duke Aycock and a rich boyfriend that owns the plane!

ROSACOKE

Tell the truth.

MILO

Bible truth. I stopped at the store to get Sim to help me in case of a crash; and before we could leave, the telephone rang—Willie's Mama called to ask for oysters: Willie's new friend wants oysters for supper. She said the family hadn't calmed down yet; said when that airplane touched ground in the pasture, every tit on the cow stood out like potlegs and streamed good milk!

Rosa stands and turns to Emma.

ROSACOKE

I'll take those clothes on down to Mary's.

MILO

Stay where you are and start grinning wide.

ROSACOKE

Milo, what do you mean?

MILO

I mean what I said—your cares are ended. If Willie marries that fool with the plane, doesn't it mean you can walk right to Wesley—no briars in the path?

ROSACOKE

You ask Wesley that.

MILO

You ask him—shortly. Wesley came home in that airplane too.

Emma sits on the bed, looks to Rosa.

Rosa stands before her mirror, puts a comb to her hair—slowly, not rushed.

ROSACOKE

Is that the truth?

MILO

(Raising a hand) It's what Mrs. Aycock said on the phone.

Rosa combs on slowly.

Emma rises.

EMMA

I'll put those clothes in a bag for you, Rosa.

MILO

She's not moving, Mama. The clothes can wait.

Milo moves to the open door, beckons Emma to precede him. She does reluctantly. Milo follows her out.

Alone, Rosa puts down her comb; moves to the mantel, studies her father's picture briefly. Then she quietly moves downstairs to the empty porch; waits on the steps, watching the road. Shifts of light show the coming of evening. A few cars pass; none stops. She shivers as a fall chill rises, holds herself close.

Behind her in the downstairs room, all gather at the table for supper.

Emma turns on a lamp at the foot of the stairs and moves to the porch.

EMMA

Rosa, come eat something.

ROSACOKE

Thank you, I couldn't.

The family eat silently behind her awhile; then Emma whispers to Baby Sister, who moves out to Rosa, a sweater in hand.

BABY SISTER

Mama sent you this.

ROSACOKE

Thank her for me. *(Puts it on carefully—not looking at Baby Sister, who waits behind)*

BABY SISTER

Someday will you explain it?

ROSACOKE

What?

BABY SISTER

What all this is for—why everybody punishes themselves like this.

ROSACOKE

You'll learn soon enough. *(Smiles)* Then explain it to me. Don't worry; you'll learn.

BABY SISTER

You could leave here, Rosa—get a job in Raleigh.

ROSACOKE

(Thinks) I could. Every worry I've got travels light as a tent though; I can pitch them anywhere.

Baby Sister stares on, shivering.

ROSACOKE

You're turning blue—go in; save your life. Might as well have one woman carry on the name.

BABY SISTER

Women don't do that.

ROSACOKE

(Nods, strokes her own shoulder) It's the one thing they don't carry *here.* Get warm.

Baby Sister goes in.

Rosa buttons the sweater, the lights and sound of a car approach, a car door slams.

Willie and Heywood Betts enter quickly.

WILLIE

Rosa, meet my aviator—Rosacoke Mustian, this is Heywood Betts, my boyfriend that flew me down.

ROSACOKE

(Smiles) How do you do?

HEYWOOD

I've dislocated my neck, I think, but otherwise working—flying's just a hobby; scrap metal's my line.

ROSACOKE

Well, good luck in it. *(Retreats a step)* And good luck, Willie. *(Gives a small half-wave, then thinks herself rude)* Come in if you can.

HEYWOOD

I doubt I can. I'm being displayed to the family tonight—little showings all up and down this road.

WILLIE

Thank you but we're stopping by Marise's. *(Waits)* I thought you'd be with Wesley.

ROSACOKE

No.

HEYWOOD

Maybe he's laid up from our pasture landing.

WILLIE

Shoot, nothing bothers Wesley that much—does it, Rosa?

ROSACOKE

No, not much.

HEYWOOD

He looked plenty bothered this afternoon when you talked me into landing in your front yard.

WILLIE

Nothing bothers Wesley. He's just not himself. *(She strains up and kisses Heywood on the ear)* In case I don't see you tomorrow, Rosa, goodbye. The three of us are flying back early tomorrow. Heywood's buying a World War I submarine—

HEYWOOD

For the scrap—

WILLIE

I'm locking you in it and drowning the key. *(She moves off quickly)*

ROSACOKE

Goodbye. *(Looks toward the house, then moves to it slowly. The family are still in the dining room, beyond Rosa's hearing)*

MILO

Yeah, but what right has she got to keep everybody she knows upset just because she fell for some poor rascal seven years ago but can't pin him down?

EMMA

She's got the right of being your sister.

BABY SISTER

Sissie, what songs did they sing at your wedding? I forgot.

MILO

Her Mama sang "Hallelujah!"—several verses.

Sissie shakes her head, disgusted.

BABY SISTER

When I get married I want "Kiss of Fire" and then "Because."

MILO

Because of what?—you said just now nobody could pay you to marry a man.

Toward the end of that, Rosa has entered and gone to the far wall to get the bag of clothes.

MILO

Where you been?

ROSACOKE

Walking.

MILO

Where you going now?

ROSACOKE

To take these clothes to Mildred's baby.

MILO

Won't me and Sissie need them?

ROSACOKE

Twenty-year-old rags?—here, keep them. Sure.

MILO

No, but you don't need to go to Mary's either—near dark and chilly.

ROSACOKE

When did you ever know anything I needed? *(Moves to leave)*

MILO

(Lets her reach the front door, then calls behind her) I know you need a good dose of Sissie's method. Sissie, tell Rosa what your old uncle said was the way to hold Milo.

SISSIE

I got you honest. My uncle never told me a word.

MILO

Yes he did.

Rosa has waited in fascinated revulsion by the door.

MILO

(Advances on her, stands stiff in parody of a child's recitation, grins and sings)

"Pull up your petticoat, pull down your drawers,
Give him a look at old Santy Claus."

Emma and Sissie cry "Milo!" together.

Baby Sister laughs.

Milo gives a schoolboy's bow to Rosa, who watches another moment; then leaves.

2

A quarter-hour later, Mary Sutton's house. A room that seems empty—a chair, a table; on the table a wooden peach crate sits waiting.

Rosa probes the emptiness by calling.

ROSACOKE

Mary? Mary, I've brought Mildred's baby some clothes. *(No sign of Mary. Rosa stands puzzled in the door, then seems to hear a sound from the peach crate, goes there. As she sets down the bag and bends to see, the baby cries. She lifts him to calm him, but the crying increases so she puts him back)* Baby, I'm not what you need. *(Moves a step to leave)*

The door is blocked by Mary.

Rosa points behind to the howling child.

ROSACOKE

Come on, Mary, and help this child.

MARY

(Unsmiling) What you done to Mildred's baby?

ROSACOKE

Not a thing—he's sick.

MARY

He ain't sick. He just passing time.

ROSACOKE

I came in to bring him these clothes and he woke up.

MARY

And you picked him up when I done just fed him?

ROSACOKE

I was trying to stop his crying, Mary. Don't get mad.

The crying is weaker. Mary enters and touches the baby. He quiets.

MARY

What you so scared of crying for? He come here crying and he be crying when I ain't here to hush him. He got his right to cry, Rosacoke; and why ain't you used to babies by now?

ROSACOKE

I will be soon. Milo's wife is overdue.

MARY

(Smiles at last) Yes'm. Sit down, Miss Rosa. Thank you for the clothes.

ROSACOKE

It's nearly night, Mary. I better get home.

MARY

You come by yourself?

ROSACOKE

Just me and my thoughts. *(Smiles)* I'll come back soon and stay longer then.

MARY

Yes'm. I know you're busy tonight. They tell me Mr. Wesley got him a plane.

ROSACOKE

News moves round here. No, that's not his plane. He just hitched a ride.

MARY

How's he coming on, Rosacoke?

ROSACOKE

Wesley?—fine, I guess. I haven't laid eyes on him since the funeral.

MARY

I didn't know that.

ROSACOKE

It's God's own truth. He's working in Norfolk, scarcer than ever. Says I got to say do I really want him. I thought I'd said it. *(Smiles with difficulty, meaning to leave; moves to the door)* Mary, what must I do?

MARY

Don't ask me—here I sit alone.

ROSACOKE

But say anyhow—everybody else has.

MARY

(Waits) He what you need? *(Rosa seems to nod)* Hold him then, if you can. All I know. *(Mary points through the door)* He's right in yonder behind them trees.

ROSACOKE

(Faces Mary another moment) Mary, excuse me.

MARY

Step along, Rosacoke, or night'll catch you.

Rosa leaves.

3

A quarter-hour later, the porch of Wesley's home.

He sits on the top step, playing his harmonica, both hands cupped round his mouth.

Rosa enters carefully, unnoticed by him, and stops five yards from the steps to listen.

He sees her and pauses.

ROSACOKE

Don't stop. *(He plays on a little, the song unfinished)* Is that all you know?

WESLEY

No. Oh no. *(Smiles)* But it's all I'm giving. Got to save my strength.

ROSACOKE

(Tries for lightness) For what?

WESLEY

My life. *(Waits, smiles again)* My pitiful life.

ROSACOKE

I heard you playing almost to Mary's. *(Points behind)* I've been to Mary's to see Mildred's baby. *(Wesley laughs gently. It whines through his harp)* If you managed everything good as you manage a harp, wouldn't none of your friends ever be upset.

WESLEY

Wesley's friends got to take Wesley—lock, stock and block—or leave him alone.

ROSACOKE

Doesn't make his friends' life easy, does it?

WESLEY

(Still smiling) Who did I beg to be my friend?

ROSACOKE

You've spent your life—or the last seven years—drawing people to you.

WESLEY

They don't have to come. I don't carry a gun.

ROSACOKE

That may well be. *(Looks up to the sky—a night sky now)* Can I use your phone? It's darker than I counted on.

WESLEY

To get home, you mean? I can carry you.

ROSACOKE

Can you? I wonder.

WESLEY

I've wondered myself.

ROSACOKE

Reached any conclusions? *(Wesley faces her plainly but does not speak)* Then while you're waiting, do me a favor—say "Rosacoke."

WESLEY

Why?

ROSACOKE

A gift to me.

WESLEY

Rosacoke.

ROSACOKE

Thank you. That's my name. Bet you haven't said it since late July.

WESLEY

(Smiles) I don't talk to trees and shrubs like some people if that's what you mean.

ROSACOKE

It's not what I mean. You're Wesley—is that still right?

WESLEY

Unless the law has changed it and not notified me.

ROSACOKE

Just checking. I know such a few facts about you that sometimes I wonder if I even know your name.

WESLEY

Yes ma'm. Rest easy. It's Wesley all right and is Wesley walking you home or not?

ROSACOKE

I'd thank you—yes.

WESLEY

And you'd be welcome. *(Reaches behind on the porch, finds a flashlight, descends toward her)* Won't cost you a cent.

Wesley offers his hand, she takes it; they leave.

Slowly they walk through changes of light—time and place. In dark spots, Wesley does not use the flashlight and makes no sound.

Rosa stops at last.

ROSACOKE

Might as well be on the motorcycle for all we've said.

WESLEY

What you want to say?

ROSACOKE

(Waits) I want to say you are half this trouble, that you've never talked to me, and now you're gone, and I don't know— *(Breaks off, shamed, in her old harangue)* I want to say I've said it *all*, till my teeth ache with shame.

WESLEY

You haven't—not all. I've answered every question the best I could, best *I* could. There's one left for you— *(A sudden crashing in the near woods halts them)* Jesus, Rosa!

ROSACOKE

Wesley!

As the sound retreats, they wait a stunned moment.

WESLEY

(Half-whispers) All my life I waited on that—

ROSACOKE

A deer? Me and Mildred saw one years ago.

WESLEY

A grown buck leading two does to water. They were killed all through here before you were born.

ROSACOKE

What water, Wesley?

WESLEY

Mr. Isaac's spring. I've seen tracks there. I scared them, talking.

ROSACOKE

Will he try again?

WESLEY

If he doesn't hear us.

ROSACOKE

We could wait.

WESLEY

You want to?

Rosa thinks a moment, nods.

They sit on a low rise and silently wait. Then the deer cross toward the spring—delicate sounds. Wesley watches closely; Rosa watches him.

A moment to realize they are gone; then Wesley moves to stand.

Rosa touches his arm.

ROSACOKE

Since it's not too cold, we could walk behind them—find the spring.

WESLEY

If you want to. We won't see the deer.

ROSACOKE

If we went gently—

Wesley studies her, takes her hand and rises. Slowly—together, silent—they move inward. Deeper darkness.

Rosa at last pulls back on his hand.

ROSACOKE

Listen.

WESLEY

To what?

ROSACOKE

I thought we might hear them. Mildred and I saw the deer we saw in a field like this.

WESLEY

Not this field.

ROSACOKE

How do you know?

WESLEY

(His voice begins to alter in speed and pitch till it gradually seems a stranger's) This is my private field. Mr. Isaac doesn't know he owns this field. Nobody knows this field but me.

ROSACOKE

I never knew it.

WESLEY

You know it now.

ROSACOKE

I know it now. *(They stand, hands joined, but she cannot see him. She begins to feel fear but tries to speak lightly)* It's night all right—dark early now. Wesley, switch on your light. I can't see you. *(She moves away)*

WESLEY

(Waits) You mean to take pictures?

ROSACOKE

No.

WESLEY

Then if you don't need light, this boy doesn't.

He offers a hand, firm but undemanding.

She stands a moment, then goes to accept it.

He sets both hands on her shoulders and presses her down.

On their knees in near-darkness, they kiss—hands at sides. Then Rosa begins to unbutton his shirt.

Wesley waits till she's finished—his chest bare to her; she lays a palm on it. He takes her wrist, pushes her gently to her back. In deeper dark, he opens his belt; slides down his pants and trousers, begins to bare Rosa. Then he lies upon her and slowly moves.

Total dark till Wesley can speak.

WESLEY

Thank you, Lady. *(He slowly rolls off, lies on his back beside her and launches a flashlight beam on the sky)* Did you know this light won't ever stop flying? Nothing to block it. Millions of years from tonight—somewhere—people in space will move in my light.

ROSACOKE

Is that something else you learned in the Navy?

WESLEY

Ain't I a good learner? *(He reaches to touch Rosa again. She seizes his wrist and holds him back)* Why?

ROSACOKE

I got to go home.

WESLEY

What you got at home as good as what's here?

Wesley takes her hand, pulls it down toward himself.

Rosa draws back and stands.

ROSACOKE

If you won't carry me, I'll gladly walk; but since you know these woods so well, please lend me your light.

WESLEY

(Sits upright, throws his light on her face, sees the baffling change) Are you all right?

ROSACOKE

I'm all right. *(Moves to leave)*

Wesley stands and puts his clothes together, then comes up behind her, shines his light at the ground.

WESLEY

You need to remember—the way you feel is a natural thing after what we've done. You answered me. The sadness'll pass. You'll feel good as you ever did. Gradually better. *(Touches her shoulder; she doesn't turn)*

ROSACOKE

We haven't done nothing. I haven't answered nothing. *(Moves on again to the bottom porch step of the Mustian house. The porch light is on. At last she turns)*

WESLEY

I'm out of my depth. Hell, Rosa, I'm drowning. Stand still and say what you want out of me.

ROSACOKE

I don't want anything you've got to give. I've just been mistaken—

SISSIE

(Inside) Help me, Milo. Help me please.

Light rises in the upstairs room—now Milo and Sissie's: Sissie in bed, Milo, Emma, Mary Sutton and Dr. Sledge silently busy round her.

ROSACOKE

Sissie's started. Please leave. *(Climbs two steps)*

WESLEY

Are you all right?

ROSACOKE

I answered that once. I was just mistaken. If that's *you,* Wesley; if that's what you've been, I've been wrong for years.

WESLEY

(Waits, nods twice) It's me *and* you.

Rosa shakes her head No, looks to the house, then quickly enters.

Wesley stands a moment, then moves away.

A long moan from Sissie.

Rosa has climbed the stairs and stands in the open door.

MILO

Thank God you're here.

Three shouts from Sissie.

Rosa watches for a long hard moment, then turns, comes quickly down and out the front door.

EMMA

Mary, see about Rosacoke.

Mary follows Rosa, stops in the front door.

MARY

(Harshly) Rosa! *(Rosa stops in the yard)* Where you running now? That girl's in trouble.

ROSACOKE

Who is she to me?

MARY

I thought you and Milo were brother and sister. It's his wife, Rosacoke—the one he picked—and whatever baby comes here tonight will be his and part yours. So where're you running?

ROSACOKE

I can't go back in that room, Mary. I'm no use there.

MARY

Then wait in the kitchen. Baby Sister's in there with Mildred's baby and Mr. Macey Gupton. They're making candy. It's going to be a long setting-up, I can tell you. Her waters've broke and she's dry as a bone.

ROSACOKE

(Moves toward the house) I need to talk to you.

MARY

About what?

ROSACOKE

I did what you said.

MARY

I never said what to do; I asked you a question. *(A new cry from Sissie, Mary turns toward the door)* I'll come down to see you if they give me a chance.

Rosa nods and follows Mary in.

The dining room lights—Baby Sister and Macey Gupton at the table.

Baby Sister reaches for fudge from a platter as Rosa enters.

ROSACOKE

Baby Sister, one sick woman is enough.

MACEY

Don't grudge her something harmless as fudge. Four years ago Marise hadn't thought about much but candy. Look at her now—got three babies out of me quick as gunshots and a fourth on the way. *(A moan from Sissie, exhausted now)* Sounds like she's dying, I know. She's not. She's doing what's as natural as skin. Some women do it easier than that. Marise has them easy as puppies—drops one, stands up, spreads the bed and cooks my supper in one afternoon.

ROSACOKE

(Not rudely) Macey, go home.

MACEY

Milo called me here. No, Marise is strong. She said to me "Stop"; said to me right after Frederick was born, "Macey, let's stop—let's rest awhile." I told her, "Marise, I've wanted a house full of children from you since the day I saw you walking to the store with an empty Coke bottle."

ROSACOKE

Wanted them for what? *(Macey turns to her, baffled)* Baby Sister, look at what time it is.

BABY SISTER

O.K., I've looked.

ROSACOKE

Then go on to bed. You've got Sunday school tomorrow.

BABY SISTER

You're not my boss. I'm waiting for the baby.

MACEY

Go to bed, Honey. They'll be regular babies in this house now.

ROSACOKE

Macey, we're tired.

Mary enters quickly, a slip of paper in her hand.

MARY

Doctor says get this medicine, Mr. Macey.

MACEY

(Studies the prescription) Hope the druggist can read this—dozens of years of education and writes like a chicken. Thank God I'm a fool. *(Takes his coat and leaves)*

Rosa looks to Mary but Mary has moved to the peach crate on the floor and squats by that—Mildred's baby. So Rosa goes to Baby Sister.

ROSACOKE

(Half-whispers) The baby's awake. Now go to bed.

BABY SISTER

(Strains to see him) What's his name?

ROSACOKE

Go on, Baby Sister.

Baby Sister goes.

Rosa moves to where Mary is arranging the baby's blanket.

ROSACOKE

Mary, what is his name?

MARY

I call him Sledge after Dr. Sledge that tried to save Mildred, but I don't know—I expect his name's Ransom. Sammy Ransom hasn't mentioned feeding him though.

Mary stands, moves to the table, sits.

Rosa remains beside the baby.

MARY

I ain't blaming Sammy. Mildred didn't know his name herself—at least, she never told me.

ROSACOKE

She didn't know. I met her in the road last February. We hadn't seen each other since summer; and we stood there saying how cold it was till it seemed we didn't have another word to say. So we said goodbye and Mildred moved and her coat swung open and there was this little new belly riding on her. I said "Mildred, what's that?" She said "Nothing but a baby." I said "Whose?" and she said "Several asked me not to say." I said "Is anybody marrying you?" She said "No hurry. Just so he come here *named.*" I said "Are you glad?" She said "*Glad* ain't got nothing to do with it, Rosa. He coming here whether I'm glad or not." *(Stands slowly, moves to the table near Mary)* Once she was gone round the bend in the road, she was gone for good. Never saw her again—not alive, not her face.

MARY

(Studies Rosa) Why are you telling me that? Mildred done what she had to do. Don't blame her now.

ROSACOKE

(Rousing from memory) Not blaming, just remembering. I've got a good memory.

MARY

Noticed you have. *(Waits)* Rosacoke, you got to live in the present.

ROSACOKE

I've been trying to—tonight. That doesn't stop me regretting Mildred—that she stretched out in the dark somewhere and took this baby from some hot boy that didn't love her, that she didn't love no more than a snake.

MARY

How old are you, child?—nearly Mildred's age, ain't you? And you still thinking and talking about *love,* still waiting round for love to strike? Time's running out on you, Rosacoke. Time's coming soon when you got to rinse your eyes and see that most people lie down and *die* without love, not the love you're talking about—two people bowing and scraping to themselves for forty years with grins on their mouths. Of course Mildred didn't love nobody like that. But she knew what she needed and took it—and it killed her. That was her hard luck. You asked me this evening what to do with Mr. Wesley; and I said if he's what you need, then hold him.

ROSACOKE

I tried that, just now. *(Points behind)* What if that shows you were wrong for years?

MARY

Wrong about what?

ROSACOKE

Who somebody was.

MARY

Then you take who they are or kill them and run. *(Smiles)*

MILO

(Runs in) Where the hell is Macey?

MARY

Gone for the medicine.

MILO

We need it now. Both of them are dying. Rosa, come on with me. We'll have to go get it.

Rosa looks to her hands, does not rise.

Milo moves to the door.

MILO

You owe me this much.

ROSACOKE

You ought to have thought of that three hours ago when you sang me your song.

Milo waits a moment, then leaves.

MARY

That was somebody needed you. Who're you going to have left?

Rosa stands and runs out.

Milo is halfway across the yard.

ROSACOKE

I beg your pardon.

MILO

Come on.

Rosa follows Milo toward the car.

Emma comes to the front door.

EMMA

Rosa—

Milo stops in his tracks, his back to the house.

Rosa moves back to Emma.

EMMA

It never breathed.

ROSACOKE

What was it?

EMMA

A boy. *(Looks to Milo, his back still turned)* God help me to tell him.

ROSACOKE

You'll freeze. I'll go to Milo.

EMMA

And stick beside him, whatever he does? You promise me that?

ROSACOKE

Yes'm. I will.

EMMA

Tell him Sissie's safe.

Rosa nods and goes toward Milo, stops six feet away.

He slightly turns.

ROSACOKE

It's over. Milo—he never even breathed.

MILO

He? Don't you know his name? He's had a name since the day I made him.

ROSACOKE

Father's name?

MILO

(Nods) That was the trouble—that and the sorry mother he had. Sissie killed him sure as if she cut him with a knife—to punish me.

ROSACOKE

Milo, that isn't so. I won't stand here and say I love Sissie, but she worked nine months to make that child, and nobody works that long in hate.

MILO

I've worked every day of my life in hate.

ROSACOKE

(Still six feet away) Milo, take that back. You don't mean that. *(He looks to the ground but never says No; so Rosa goes to him, encircles him from behind, lays her head against him, talks from there)* I'll help you any way I can, any way you need. *(Waits, no reply)* We could take a ride. Or a walk up the road. It's not that cold. When you were a boy, let you be worried, you'd walk for miles—remember that? *(No reply. Milo looks to the house)* Let's walk to Mr. Isaac's and back. That's what we need.

Milo stares on at the house, then gently walks from Rosa's arms toward the porch, stops four steps away.

MILO

What I need to do and got to do are two different things. But thank you, Rosa.

Rosa stands awhile—exhausted, abandoned. Then she slowly enters the silent house, climbs to her room, removes her sweater, walks to the window, stares at the night. Her face is blank; she holds herself and shudders slightly.

ACT THREE

1

The Mustian dining room, noon, a Sunday in late December.

Baby Sister stands at the window; Sissie behind her is setting the table.

In her dim room above, Rosa stands ironing.

SISSIE

All this family does is wait. Waiting can kill you; I know. Know well. Come here and help me, Baby Sister.

BABY SISTER

(Waits, then patiently explains) Sissie, Rato's our brother that we haven't seen for nine long months—so nobody's waiting idle today and nobody's dying.

SISSIE

Rosacoke is dying—or going to die if she goes on shut up in that cold room another month like she's done this past. Ironing, *ironing*—you'd think she was running an orphanage, all the ironing she does. How come she can't do it down here with the humans?

BABY SISTER

He's here! *(Runs to the foot of the stairs, calls up)* Mama! Rosa! Rato is home! *(Runs to the yard and waves at the distance)*

EMMA

(Enters from the back of the house, takes a sweater from a hook at the foot of the stairs, calls up) Rosa? *(No reply)* Rosa, Rato is home. *(Looks into the room where Sissie still putters)* Rato is home.

SISSIE

Heard he was. Won't Rosa come down?

EMMA

Rosa is a grown woman. I don't know.

As Emma reaches the yard, Rato and Milo appear—Rato in a wrinkled uniform, Milo carrying his duffle.

EMMA

(Stops short of Rato) Welcome home, Son. Are you feeling good?

Emma opens her arms but Rato looks past her to Rosa's window.

Rosa stands looking down, grave like Milo.

Emma touches Rato's shoulders to brush him off, strains up to kiss his neck.

EMMA

You're feeling fine. You've put on weight.

RATO

Army food. Rosa sick? *(No response. He looks to all the faces)* Sick with what?

EMMA

She's all right—just the Christmas dumps.

BABY SISTER

(Quickly to Rato) Everybody tells me I'm too young but I know Rosa is not herself—comes home from work, climbs to her room, lies there staring, or washes and irons clothes she washed the night before. She hasn't even eaten since Friday night.

EMMA

No, I took her something. *(Takes Rato's arm)* You'll cheer her up.

RATO

I'll help anybody if they tell me what's wrong. *(Looks up again)*

Rosa gives a little wave, half-beckoning; then goes back to ironing.

MILO

(Gently) You try it. Everybody else has lost.

They all go in. Rato climbs at once to Rosa's, opens without knocking, stands on the sill.

ROSACOKE

(In place) Merry Christmas, Rato.

RATO

(Moves to her, holds out his hand to touch. Rosa takes it a moment) Merry Christmas yourself. What you doing up here?

ROSACOKE

(Smiles at last, shrugs) I live up here.

RATO

(Looks round the too-neat room—the only disorder, a pile of rough laundry on the bed) You taking in wash?

ROSACOKE

(Shutting the door behind him) No, I just seem to use a lot of clothes.

RATO

Ought to join the Army—just have the one suit of clothes on your back.

ROSACOKE

(Laughing) Rato, that's not so.

RATO

(Nods, walks to Rosa's mantel, studies the picture of their father, then reaches beside it and takes up a picture that is laid facedown) You ought to get a new one—he's changed so much. *(Shows her the large tenth-grade picture of Wesley)*

ROSACOKE

(Moves to the ironing board) I don't think so.

RATO

He has though. *(Replaces the picture)* Rosa, when are your plans?

ROSACOKE

There aren't any plans.

RATO

You and Wesley, I mean.

ROSACOKE

(Trying for lightness) The morning after Judgment Day. There aren't any plans.

RATO

I thought you had him.

Rosa wants to answer fully but can only shake her head.

Both stand steady, hands at their sides.

RATO

You told me years ago he'd be your life. We were back in the woods—Milo had left us. You asked me what was a happy life; and I said "For people to let me alone"; but you said your idea was marrying Wesley and having some children that would look like him and have his name but be half yours and answer when you call—and for that to last as long as you lasted. You forgot that? *(Rosa shakes her head)* Don't forget it. It's all in the world you know how to do. The *world's* solid fools. I'm the one in this family that's traveled so listen to me.

Rosa faces him but cannot reply.

BABY SISTER

(From the foot of the stairs) Rato, dinner is ready.

RATO

(Half-whispers) Dinner is ready.

ROSACOKE

I can't eat a mouthful.

RATO

I've eaten just peanuts since Friday—come on. *(She shakes her head)* What's wrong with you?

ROSACOKE

I've got Wesley's baby.

RATO

Good. *(She shakes her head)* Why not? Does Wesley know?

ROSACOKE

I don't want Wesley.

RATO

Why?

ROSACOKE

He doesn't want me.

RATO

You don't know that. You're hard on people, Rosa. We're not as quick as you. Tell him now and wait till he answers.

Through that, the family has gathered in the dining room. Baby Sister calls again.

BABY SISTER

Rato—

RATO

Tell him. *(Offers his hand)* And come on with me. I've worked to see you. You're the one here I like.

Rosa thinks, half-smiles, takes his hand, and they go. In the dining room, all quickly sit at the table and bow for grace.

EMMA

Lord, make us thankful for Your many blessings. *(All mutter "Amen," begin to pass dishes)* Son, do you have a chaplain for the Baptists or does everybody get the same one?

RATO

Haven't seen a Baptist since early April. Just Catholics.

EMMA

You'll see some tonight.

RATO

Where?

BABY SISTER

The church—we're having the Christmas pageant and you're in it.

RATO

No I'm not.

MILO

Yes you are. Me and you're Wise Men.

RATO

Are you in it, Rosa?

ROSACOKE

No, I was Mary last year—remember?

RATO

If you're not, I'm not.

MILO

Yes you are. I'm the head Wise Man. You're my helper.

BABY SISTER

Who's the third?

Embarrassed silence.

Rosa stands, takes the empty biscuit plate and speaks to Rato.

ROSACOKE

The third one is Wesley, if he comes in time. *(Moves to the kitchen)*

EMMA

(Whispers to Milo) Is Wesley here yet?

MILO

(Still chewing, face down) He's here. I saw him when I went to get Rato.

EMMA

What did he say?

MILO

He said was he welcome in this house still?

EMMA

What did you say?

MILO

Mama, Rosacoke is not my business. *(Waits)* I said "What do you mean?" Wesley said he had written to her three times since that weekend in early November—even asked her to visit him in Norfolk at Thanksgiving—but he hadn't heard a word.

EMMA

What did you say to that?

MILO

I said "You're no more confused than us. Rosa lives above us—takes up bed space, breathes the same air—but for three weeks now, she's a stranger to us."

EMMA

Did you tell him he was still welcome though?

MILO

I don't think he is—not with her, not now. Anyhow, I've given my last advice. Nothing I said ever helped anybody.

Rosa reappears from the kitchen with a heaped plate of biscuits and goes to serve Rato.

RATO

When is Christmas?

ROSACOKE

Wednesday. *(Goes to her chair)*

EMMA

You anxious, Son?

Rato suddenly stands, rushes to the foot of the stairs, finds his duffle, brings it in and squats to search it.

BABY SISTER

Did you bring your gun?

RATO

No, I brought everybody presents from the PX. Everything's cheap there.

EMMA

That's fine, Son, but wait till Wednesday.

RATO

No ma'm. We all could be sick by Wednesday.

He finds a few boxes tied with ribbon, weighs them in his hand; gives one to Baby Sister, who opens it quickly—and brandishes a baby-toy: a large elephant. She is plainly embarrassed.

BABY SISTER

Thank you, Rato.

RATO

(Still squatting) That's O.K.

EMMA

That's nice, Sister. That can be your mascot.

RATO

(Stands, sees the elephant, seizes it back) This wasn't yours. I got it mixed-up.

Sissie's face clenches but she tries to hold on.

Silent pain is visible on all.

RATO

Listen. I bought all this back before Thanksgiving. I'll have to check it. I forgot what's what.

Sissie rises carefully and leaves.

Rato watches her, puzzled.

EMMA

Sit down, Son, and finish your dinner. Christmas is coming; everybody's just tired.

RATO

Amen to that.

MILO

(Quietly) Hallelujah, Amen.

2

A quarter-hour later, the Mustian dining room. Rosa and Emma clear the table quietly. A distant car passes.

EMMA

Whose car was that?

ROSACOKE

Macey Gupton's.

EMMA

Headed to church? *(Rosa nods. Emma glances to a clock on the mantel)* Lord, it's time for pageant practice and Macey's beating me.

ROSACOKE

Getting Marise there in plenty of time.

EMMA

Marise isn't Mary after all—didn't I tell you? She stopped me yesterday morning at the store and said she just felt too big now but that she knew Willie would gladly fill in. I knew it too but I waited as late as I could for you. Then when you didn't feel any better this morning, I tried to reach Willie. *(She has roused no sign of interest in Rosa but continues nervously)* Her mother said

Willie and Heywood had gone for a little ride—at nine in the morning—but that she knew Willie would be proud to serve. So Willie gets her chance after all these years—maybe God will forgive me before I die! Frederick Gupton is Jesus and I hope he's tired enough to shut up tonight.

The sound of another car.

Rosa moves toward the window to see.

Emma waits a moment, comes up behind her, reaches to touch her shoulder but doesn't.

EMMA

Rosacoke, you're my smartest child; and I've never claimed to understand you, but I know one thing—we're well into winter and you've barely laughed since summer ended. I know some reasons but I doubt I know all; and even if you are mine, I won't ask anything you don't need to tell. I just want to say, if you've got any kind of trouble needs telling—I'm your mother at least. Nobody else is. *(Rosa does not turn)* If there's anybody you don't want to see at the pageant tonight, stay at home; I won't make you go. I understand. *(Rosa slowly shakes her head No)* What does that mean?

ROSACOKE

(Facing the road) That you don't understand.

EMMA

Tell me then. Now.

ROSACOKE

You said you wouldn't ask.

EMMA

I lied. I'm asking.

ROSACOKE

(Turning, tired but calm) I'll tell you when I get home from work tomorrow.

EMMA

You don't know for sure?

ROSACOKE

I know, yes ma'm.

EMMA

Is there somebody you need to tell before me?

ROSACOKE

I halfway thought so. As usual he's absent.

EMMA

He's not. He's a half-mile away—a few bare trees.

ROSACOKE

That's the moon to me.

EMMA

Then you put him there. He's one local boy. Let me speak to him now; I'll see him at practice.

ROSACOKE

Do and I'll die. This is my thing, Mama.

EMMA

Yours and one other human's, if I understand.

ROSACOKE

You don't understand.

EMMA

It's not the first time. Will I tomorrow evening?

ROSACOKE

You'll know tomorrow evening.

EMMA

(Stands a long moment, unable to touch her) I've got to go now. *(Moves to the door)* Why don't you fix up and walk to Mr. Isaac's?—take him his Christmas candy early. You've carried candy to him every Christmas since your father died.

ROSACOKE

(Nods Yes but speaks to the window) I know my duties.

EMMA

I'm praying you do. *(Leaves slowly, Rosa still at the window)*

Rosa stays in place a moment, then moves to the foot of the stairs; takes her coat, a paper sack tied with green ribbon; walks out and slowly to Mr. Isaac Alston's door: knocks three times.

Sammy comes in clean work clothes. At first he seems not to recognize her.

SAMMY

Rosacoke. I didn't know you. How're you getting on?

ROSACOKE

Kicking—but not high, Sammy.

SAMMY

I hope you improve by Christmas. Step in.

ROSACOKE

No, I'll head on back. But I won't be going to church this evening, so I brought Mr. Isaac his Christmas candy. *(Offers the sack)*

SAMMY

(Reaches to take it, then draws back) You give it to him. He needs some company.

ROSACOKE

What he'll need is rest if he's going to the pageant.

SAMMY

(Gestures inward) He don't do nothing but rest, Rosacoke. It's near about all he lives for now—horehound candy and going to ride and company. You be his company this afternoon.

Rosa enters with Sammy. They move to a room where Mr. Isaac sits in a chair, neatly dressed—no tie but his collar buttoned at the neck. He is chewing slowly.

Sammy goes to him, sits him up straighter.

SAMMY

This is your friend, Rosacoke, Mr. Isaac. Tell her Merry Christmas.

MR. ISAAC

(Stares at her closely) Merry Christmas. *(He chews some white mass)*

SAMMY

What in the world you eating now? *(Presses Mr. Isaac's lower jaw down, coaxes him gently)* Spit it out, Mr. Isaac—that ain't candy; that's soap. *(Mr. Isaac spits the mass into Sammy's palm)* Now you sit here and talk to Rosacoke while I get you something to rinse your mouth else you'll be blowing bubbles at the Christmas pageant. Sit here, Miss Rosa. *(Draws a straight chair close to Mr. Isaac's. Rosa comes to it, stands)* There's a lot worse things than dying, Rosacoke. How's Miss Sissie?

ROSACOKE

She's out of bed now. Her mind's still tender.

SAMMY

Wasn't it a boy? What was his name?

ROSACOKE

It would've been Horatio, after our father.

SAMMY

I hope they get them a new one soon.

ROSACOKE

I don't know if they could stand it again.

SAMMY

People not having much luck this year. *(Waits)* Have you seen Mildred's baby?

ROSACOKE

Yes, more than once.

SAMMY

Don't he take after Mildred? I saw him last week. Miss Mary

had him at the church, don't you know; and I seen him—first time.

ROSACOKE

Sammy, I better go—

SAMMY

Please sit with him while I get some water. Give him his candy. *(Rosa nods, Sammy goes)*

ROSACOKE

(Sits, pulls the ribbon off the sack, offers it open) Merry Christmas, Mr. Isaac—and many more.

MR. ISAAC

(His good hand enters the sack) I will. I can't die. If you were to shoot me, I wouldn't die.

ROSACOKE

I won't shoot you then.

Mr. Isaac loudly crushes one piece of candy, chews it slowly.

Rosa moves to rise.

With shocking speed, his good hand takes her wrist and presses her down. Then he studies her hand.

MR. ISAAC

Who are you?

ROSACOKE

I'm Rosacoke—Horatio and Emma Mustian's girl. You've known me all my life.

MR. ISAAC

Are the children here?

ROSACOKE

No, Mr. Isaac. I'm as single as you.

MR. ISAAC

Why?

ROSACOKE

(Trying for lightness) Why are you?

MR. ISAAC

(Releases her hand) Nobody ever asked me to change. *(Smiles, his mouth full of candy)*

ROSACOKE

(Half-smiling) That's most people's reason.

MR. ISAAC

And most people live and die in misery. *(Chews on awhile)* I do not understand.

ROSACOKE

Well, don't ask me. I'm twenty. *(Waits, then hopes to change the drift)* I hear you're going to church this evening.

MR. ISAAC

(Nods) I go every time they open the door but I don't pray. If I can't die, how come I should pray? *(Points to a spot on the bare floor)* I don't pray no more than that dog does yonder.

Held by his force, Rosa follows the point for a moment; then rises.

ROSACOKE

I better be—

MR. ISAAC

I'll give you a nickel to scratch my head.

ROSACOKE

(Sees a brush) I'll brush it for you.

She sets the sack of candy in his lap, takes the brush, stands behind him and begins to brush with short timid strokes.

Then as she eases into the job, he seems to doze.

Rosa pauses then and stares out his window, more nearly at peace than for six weeks past.

MR. ISAAC

(Eyes still shut, not moving beneath her hand) Tell me who you are. I'll remember you.

ROSACOKE

I'm one of Emma Mustian's children that you've been seeing for twenty years—passing in the road or back in the woods at your spring or at church—so if you don't know by now, it must not be your fault.

At that, Wesley knocks on Mr. Isaac's front door.

Sammy goes; they exchange an inaudible greeting. Then Sammy waves him in, and they move toward Mr. Isaac's room as Rosa continues.

ROSACOKE

I've changed till I hardly know myself. Been changed by a boy I thought I wanted—

SAMMY

I got *you* a present, Rosacoke.

WESLEY

(Tentatively) Merry Christmas, Rosa.

ROSACOKE

(Surfaces slowly from reverie) Why have you trailed me?

WESLEY

Your mother sent me home to get you. Sissie said you were here. Willie's eloped with Heywood Betts, and you've got to be in the pageant tonight, so they need you to practice.

ROSACOKE

No.

She strains at control but intends to leave; she takes two steps around Mr. Isaac's chair.

He claws at her coat.

She stops to listen.

He urgently holds the sack of candy toward her.

MR. ISAAC

Give this to the children.

Rosa stares at the candy in baffled fear.

SAMMY

(Leans to Mr. Isaac, tries to take the candy) What children, Mr. Isaac? This is Rosacoke and that's your candy, your Christmas present.

MR. ISAAC

(Clutches the candy, still offers it to Rosa) This is for the children. Say it's from me. They were good to me.

Rosa shakes her head slowly as if a paralysis were flooding her. Then she gives a low groan and runs from the room—out the front door, Wesley a few strides behind her.

At the edge of the yard, he touches her shoulder.

She stops there, beyond him.

WESLEY

Please tell me what hurts you.

ROSACOKE

Nothing you can cure.

WESLEY

You don't know that. *I* don't know that till you tell me the trouble.

ROSACOKE

It's *my* trouble and if you don't know by now—

WESLEY

I don't know anything about you, Rosa; and I've know you seven years. Six weeks ago you welcomed me, then turned yourself like a weapon against me—won't answer my letters, won't tell me nothing. You don't have the right. *(With both hands he takes her arms at the elbows, holds her firmly but gently)* We've got to go practice. Everybody's waiting. Come on with me. *(Rosa shakes her head No)* Rosa, Willie has gone. You've got to take her part or your mother's show will fail.

ROSACOKE

Marise Gupton can do it.

WESLEY

You haven't seen Marise lately then. She's the size of that house. *(Points behind him, glances back)*

Sammy stands in the door.

Wesley waves him in.

WESLEY

It's all right, Sammy.

Sammy nods and goes.

ROSACOKE

It's not all right.

WESLEY

(Still behind her, he reaches for her left hand. She lets him hold it) Why?

ROSACOKE

(Frees her hand; turns to face him, calm but tired) Marise Gupton is not the only person working on a child.

WESLEY

Who do you mean?

ROSACOKE

I mean Rosacoke.

WESLEY

(Thinks a long moment) And Wesley then. *(Rosa shakes her head No, not fiercely but firmly. With his hand in the air, he asks her to*

wait) Understand this one thing and answer—you don't know nobody but me, do you?

ROSACOKE

I don't know you.

WESLEY

Don't lie to me—you know what's here. *(Waits)* You don't know anybody else, do you, Rosa?

ROSACOKE

You know I don't.

WESLEY

(Draws one long breath, slowly exhales it; makes no try to touch her again but extends his offer in a mild half-whisper) Come on then. We got to go practice. *(He turns to go and has gone four steps before he knows he is walking alone. He stops and half-turns. Rosa is facing her home but has not moved. Wesley comes back to her; by now his voice is almost happy)* Rosa, why didn't you tell me sooner?

ROSACOKE

What good would that have done?

WESLEY

Good?—maybe not. But it would've been fair.

ROSACOKE

I can't see I owe you two more words.

WESLEY

Try one. Try *Wesley*. Wesley's my name.

ROSACOKE

(Smiles) I'll try to remember that. *(Takes a homeward step, turns) Weapons,* Wesley—I have lain down and got up and worked through years with you driven into my chest like a nail.

Wesley takes that, full face; then slowly comes toward her, begins quietly as if to himself.

WESLEY

Rosa, you aren't the only human made out of skin. What do you think us others are? What do you think I've been these long years?—asbestos? wood? I'm not, not now if I ever was. I may not have talked as well as you. Or planned as far. I may have disappointed you hundreds of times, but I'm still the person you claimed to love and plan a life on. I've shied from plans. *(Waits)* I'm not shying now. We'll leave here after the pageant tonight and be in South Carolina by day—we won't need a license; that's where everybody goes. We can spend a night somewhere, be back by Christmas eve—

ROSACOKE

I'm not everybody. I'm just the cause of this one baby. It's mine—something really mine from the start; I'll have it on my own.

WESLEY

And shame your mother and feed it how and tell it what? Not a hundred percent yours, it's not. Remember that along with my name. *(Rosa watches him closely but doesn't answer)* Do something about me. Tell me "Go" or "Stay." *(Silence still)* We can live. I've paid up all my debts; every penny I make from here on is mine.

ROSACOKE

(Genuinely thinking aloud) Let me get this straight. You offer to drive me to South Carolina and marry me at dawn in some poor justice of the peace's living room, then give me a little one-day vacation and bring me home for Christmas with my family that will be cut again by this second blow, then take me on to Norfolk to spend my life shut in two rented rooms while you sell motorcycles—me waiting out my baby, sick and alone, eating what we could afford and pressing your shirts and staring out a window in my spare time at concrete roads and people that look like they hate each other—That's what you're standing here, offering me, after all these years?

WESLEY

Yes. It was all I ever had to offer. I never said I was anything but Wesley. All the rest you made up yourself and hung on me. Sure, that's one way of seeing my plan; but if everybody looked at their chances like that, people would have gone out of style long ago.

ROSACOKE

Maybe they should've.

WESLEY

You don't mean that.

ROSACOKE

I think I do. I haven't been sleeping.

WESLEY

You're talking like the old Wesley now.

ROSACOKE

You said there was just one Wesley all along.

WESLEY

(Shakes his head slightly) There's Wesleys you never dreamed of, Rosa.

ROSACOKE

(Opens her mouth to answer, finds only a kernel of what seems knowledge) That may be so. But—look—I'm free. I'm standing here seeing you and, Wesley, I'm free.

WESLEY

You're wrong. And I'm sorry. We've got till tonight. Believe I'm serious—whatever it means weeks or years from now—and tell me tonight. *(Rosa starts to answer)* Please. Tonight.

As Rosa faces him—silent, not moving—a piano begins to play "Joy to the World."

After six bars Rosa moves toward the sound; Wesley follows.

When the light has dimmed, Baby Sister—hidden—sings the whole first stanza.

BABY SISTER

"Joy to the world! The Lord is come!
Let earth receive her king;
Let every heart prepare Him room,
And heaven and nature sing."

3

The same night, Delight Church.

Low light on Baby Sister dressed as an angel, completing the song, "... and nature sing." She stands above a huddle of adolescent shepherds.

Then we see Rosa as Mary at the manger, Macey Gupton as Joseph behind her.

Dark at one side, Mr. Isaac in his chair with Sammy beside him.

On the other side a choir, not robed, consisting of Emma, Sissie, Marise Gupton and others.

REV. VEREEN

(Unseen) "Now when Jesus was born in Bethlehem of Judaea in the days of Herod the King, behold, there came Wise Men from the east to Jerusalem, saying—"

RATO

(Unseen at the back) "Where is he that is born King of the Jews?"

MILO

(Unseen) "For we have seen his star in the east—"

WESLEY

(Unseen, a pause) "And are come to worship him."

Piano plays a brief introduction; then all the Wise Men sing together, dark at the back.

WISE MEN

"We three Kings of Orient are.
Bearing gifts we traverse afar,

Field and fountain, moor and mountain,
Following yonder star."

Rosa is staring closely at the manger—Frederick Gupton.

The choir joins the Wise Men for each refrain.

WISE MEN AND CHOIR

"O star of wonder, star of night,
Star with royal beauty bright,
Westward leading, still proceeding,
Guide us to thy perfect light."

Rato moves forward with long slow steps in time to his solo verse.

Rosa watches him closely.

RATO

"Born a babe on Bethlehem's plain,
Gold I bring to crown Him again,
King forever, ceasing never
Over us all to reign."

As the choir, Milo and Wesley sing the refrain, Rato reaches the manger and—no flicker of recognition to Rosa, though his eyes fix on her—kneels to present his gift: a brass bowl. Then he stands aside.

CHOIR, MILO, WESLEY

"O star of wonder, star of night,
Star with royal beauty bright,
Westward leading, still proceeding,
Guide us to thy perfect light."

Milo moves forward, faster than his own verse; slows only as he kneels, presents his gift (a small wood chest) and sees the baby. His face clouds painfully.

Rosa watches through the refrain.

MILO

"Frankincense to offer have I;
Incense owns a Deity nigh.
Prayer and praising all men raising,
Worship Him, God on high."

CHOIR AND WESLEY

"O star of wonder, star of night,
Star with royal beauty bright,
Westward leading, still proceeding,
Guide us to thy perfect light."

Milo stands aside with Rato, and Wesley moves forward.

WESLEY

"Myrrh is mine. Its bitter perfume
Breathes a life of gathering gloom—
Sorrowing, sighing, bleeding, dying,
Sealed in the stone-cold tomb."

CHOIR, RATO, MILO

"O star of wonder, star of night,
Star with royal beauty bright,
Westward leading, still proceeding,
Guide us to thy perfect light."

As the choir begins the last refrain, Wesley kneels with his gift—a glass butter dish.

He meets Rosa's eyes for a moment at first; but Frederick whimpers, then begins to cry, and Rosa looks to him.

Macey leans from behind her, whispers to lift him.

As Wesley rises to join the other Wise Men, Rosa lifts Frederick and holds him through the rest. Her growing decision is firmed by two things—Frederick in her arms and the strange familiar face of Wesley, her choice from the faces of all her life, as he kneels a second time when the Wise Men leave.

REV. VEREEN

(Unseen) "Mary kept all these things and pondered them in her heart. And the shepherds returned, glorifying and praising God for all the things that they had heard and seen. . . . The Wise Men, warned of God in a dream that they should not return to Herod, departed into their own country another way. And when they were departed, behold, the angel of the Lord appeareth to Joseph in a dream, saying—"

BABY SISTER

(To Macey) "Arise, and take the young child and his mother, and flee into Egypt and be thou there until I bring thee word."

Macey helps Rosa to stand in place with Frederick.

The piano briefly introduces "Silent Night." The choir sings the necessary verses while the recessional proceeds—shepherds bowing in a group to Rosa; Rato and Milo separately and slower, Wesley last.

He fixes on Rosa's face but cannot catch her eye.

She is deep in her part still, studying Frederick.

Wesley rises and leaves—no sign of emotion.

The choir files off in increasing dark—one light remains on Rosa and Frederick, Macey dark behind them.

Rosa faces out now, firm and clear, but shows no answer.

CHOIR

"Silent night, holy night—
All is calm, all is bright
Round yon Virgin Mother and Child,
Holy Infant so tender and mild.
Sleep in heavenly peace,
Sleep in heavenly peace."

4

A quarter-hour later, Delight churchyard.

Marise Gupton comes out of the church in a winter coat—a cold night. She holds Frederick closely and speaks to him frankly as to an adult.

MARISE

You did all right. Jesus cried more than once, in my Bible anyhow.

Rosa comes out, approaches Marise.

ROSACOKE

He did fine, didn't he?

MARISE

He did all right.

ROSACOKE

I thought I'd scared him that one time though.

MARISE

(To Frederick) He may've had a bad dream. He still dreams a lot.

Macey comes out, joins them, speaks to Frederick gently.

MACEY

You all but ruined it—Rosa handled you though. *(Looks up)* Thank you, Rosa. *(Smiles)* Want to take him for Christmas? We could use some relief.

ROSACOKE

(Smiles also) So could I, Macey. My hands are full—

MACEY

Most people's are. *(Puts his arm around Marise to lead her off)* Well, Merry Christmas. *(Rosa nods)* Tell Rosacoke "Merry Christmas," Marise.

MARISE

(Looking up vaguely, finding Rosa's face) We'll be thinking of you, Rosa.

As the Guptons leave, Wesley comes out—suit and tie—and faces Rosa across a wide gap. They are gravely silent, looking still.

Emma, Baby Sister, Rato, Milo and Sissie come out.

Emma steps forward slightly, looks a moment.

EMMA

Rosacoke, are you coming with us?

Rosa looks to Wesley.

He turns to Emma.

WESLEY

I can carry her.

EMMA

You promise?

WESLEY

Promise.

EMMA

You've failed me before.

WESLEY

I may again. But not this time.

EMMA

(Waits, then nods, half-waves) Be careful. Merry Christmas. *(Turns slowly to leave)*

ROSACOKE

(In place but suddenly) That's Wednesday. Wait till Wednesday—

Emma waits a moment, nods, gives her little wave again, and goes.

Rato, Baby Sister, Milo and Sissie follow quietly—only Rato and Sissie waving.

To their vanishing backs, Rosa gives one broad gesture—farewell, gentle banishment—ending at her mouth: an instant of grief.

WESLEY

(In place) I can carry you. *(His hand comes slightly up, offered not extended)*

ROSACOKE

Why should you want to?

Wesley does not speak but his hand stays out, his calm gaze holds.

Rosa studies him a moment—face and hand—then goes to him.

Separate, a step apart, they leave together.

PRIVATE CONTENTMENT

FOR

JEFFREY ANDERSON

Private Contentment was conceived in response to a commission from WNET-Channel 13, New York. The job was to produce a ninety-minute play for television broadcast in the premiere season of the *American Playhouse* series on PBS. I wrote it in the summer and early fall of 1981. Though it is set in North Carolina, it was filmed on location in South Carolina in February 1982 and was first shown throughout the country on 27 April 1982.

The text printed here is nearly identical with the production script—differing only in the restoration of a few cuts, in a handful of minor matters affected by weather and other exigencies of filming, and in the odd small verbal change.

Recent productions have shown that the play also lends itself to the stage. With the possible omission of scenes 9 and 14, the insertion of an interval after scene 13, the use of a fluid set and a strict refusal by all parties to purvey the stereotypes of the stage-South, these characters and their actions move quite naturally into the theater.

R.P.

CHARACTERS

SGT. DI LUCCA - *a large Italian-American, mid- to late 20s*

LOGAN MELTON - *age 20, sensibly built but vulnerable*

THE CHAPLAIN - *mature with the businessman-air of Protestant clerics*

TEE - *black, late 30s, a harder edge than the traditional maid*

PAUL MELTON - *age 45, clearly once-handsome with strong remnants of his young magnetism. A decent man in possession of numerous sealed and dangerous compartments*

MR. APPLEGATE - *mid-50s, a furniture dealer*

LENA BROCK - *age 38, self-possessed but capable of surprise*

DAYTON
ADELE
TALLER BOY } *sixth-grade pupils, age 12*

GAIL BROCK - *age 14, lovely with the trace of a resemblance to Logan*

SILENT - *two men on street (one black), schoolchildren, the driver of a car*

PLACES

A military base in Idaho and eastern North Carolina

TIME

March 1945

SCENES

1. *Officers' Quarters, Idaho*
2. *The chaplain's office, Idaho*
3. *Tee's house, North Carolina*
4. *The cemetery*
5. *The Melton kitchen*
6. *The Melton porch*
7. *A furniture store*
8. *The bank of a river*
9. *A small town, Main Street*
10. *A schoolhouse*
11. *Lena's porch*
12. *Lena's garden*
13. *Lena's kitchen*
14. *Paul's car*
15. *The woods near Lena's*
16. *Lena's dining room, kitchen, pantry and front porch*
17. *The woods near Lena's*
18. *Lena's backyard*
19. *Lena's dining room*
20. *The woods near Lena's*
21. *Lena's backyard*
22. *Lena's kitchen*
23. *Lena's living room*

1

A barn of a recreation room in Officers' Quarters, U.S. Army. Idaho; late afternoon.

The hand of a young man suspends above a keyboard—old piano ivory. The fingers are slowly rehearsing in the air.

Then an unseen voice from some yards behind—

SGT. DI LUCCA

Make it sweet, Lieutenant.

The hand descends and begins to play the simplest great music, Bach's Prelude in C.

After three measures we see the whole man, earnestly recalling the piece. He is twenty, with spacious calm features and distinction in his eyes.

The heavyset sergeant approaches through the room, then stops to listen.

After ten measures the right hand misstrikes a note and stops. The lieutenant turns to face Di Lucca, smiling.

LOGAN

Maybe I'll do better under Nipponese fire.

DI LUCCA

I hope you get the chance, sir.

LOGAN

(Thinks a moment, stands) Have I overlooked a duty?

DI LUCCA

You're wanted by the chaplain, sir.

LOGAN

Hell, he wants us *all.*

DI LUCCA

Not me, sir. He's terrified of Catholics. *(Grins)* Join us.

LOGAN

Where do I sign?

Di Lucca extends a hand and Logan mock-signs it. Di Lucca studies his palm, then wipes it on his trouser leg.

DI LUCCA

You got to see him, sir. On the double, I think.

LOGAN

(Fans his arms, helpless) He's the bad-news man. *(Looks quickly out a sunny window—more soldiers walking)* Well, thanks. Maybe thanks.

Logan trots toward the door. The moment he vanishes—

DI LUCCA

Maybe you're welcome.

2

Ten minutes later, the chaplain's office.

The stout bald chaplain sits behind a desk.

Logan sits on his left, telephone in hand. He has talked with his father for several minutes now.

LOGAN

Did she have any warning? *(We do not hear his father's replies, only Logan's spaced questions and final promise)* Was she in much pain? . . . Was anybody with her? . . . I'm glad of that much . . . The chaplain says I can get a week's leave. Now I have to hop a flight. That may take a day or two . . . Are you all right? . . . I'll *be* there, Dad. *(Hangs up slowly and sits back stunned)* This morning she was sitting with the maid in the kitchen and bent to pick up a spoon off the floor. The maid said she got the spoon and clutched it but never sat up. She just kept gently going on down till she'd laid herself out. Then she hit her forehead one time with her fist. *(Repeats her action)*

CHAPLAIN

A stroke. A great blessing.

LOGAN

(Thinks, then stands) Sir, it would take more time than I've got to understand that. *(Moves toward the door, then turns)* She was still a young woman.

CHAPLAIN

(Nods) You loved her, I'm sure. *(Waits)* Shall we pray?

LOGAN

No sir.

3

Logan's hometown in North Carolina, two evenings later, falling late-winter light.

Logan has driven Tee, the family cook, home at the end of the funeral day.

Though Tee is only forty, straight and strong, Logan helps her from the car and walks beside her uphill toward the house.

When they reach the steps, Tee stops and faces him. She still wears her mourning dress and hat.

TEE

You all right, aren't you?

LOGAN

(Nods) Tired.

TEE

How many days you got to rest?

LOGAN

Five, maybe four. *(Smiles)* Then I might invade Japan.

TEE

Don't scare people, Logan. It's been a bad week.

LOGAN

(Nods) I'll be shipped out any day. You may have another funeral to cook.

TEE

(Firmly lays her palm on his lips) Don't say that anywhere your daddy can hear.

LOGAN

He never needed me.

TEE

You're what he's *got* now.

LOGAN

(Smiles) Uncle Sam's got me. Don't lean on me.

Tee reaches to stop his mouth again, but Logan takes a step back in gathering darkness.

4

Ten minutes later, the cemetery.

Logan steps from the car and walks toward his mother's grave. The funeral wreaths, left hours ago, are startlingly fresh. Logan stands a long moment, looking down. He bends, takes one red rose and smells it, then speaks to his mother.

LOGAN

I can honestly say I'm sorry you're gone. But please—I don't want to join you, not yet. Help me through what's coming. I want a whole life. *(Puts the rose to his mouth, then throws it gently to the grave)* I'm sorry you didn't but I already said that.

He turns toward the car.

5

A quarter-hour later, the kitchen of Logan's family home.

His father, Paul Melton, is seated at a clean table, a glass of bourbon before him. He is forty-five, a little fatigued but still firm and focused in body and eyes. At the sight of Logan, Paul points to a cupboard.

PAUL

You want to pour it?

LOGAN

(Moving to the cupboard) Thank you, I can.

Through the start of their talk, Logan finds ice cubes and pours a stiff glass of unwatered bourbon. He leans on a counter, facing his father but some yards distant.

PAUL

You stop by Marian's?

LOGAN

No sir, I spoke to her outside the church.

PAUL

I hoped you might have more to say to her.

LOGAN

(Smiling but earnest) Dad, I'm in the midst of a little task called World War II. If I concentrate, I may outlast it with all my parts. Then I'll start back listening to anybody offering plans for my life.

PAUL

You'll be all right.

LOGAN

You write to Hirohito? He promise to spare me?

PAUL

(Smiles) They don't, as a rule, wipe a whole family out. They wouldn't take you right after your mother.

LOGAN

"They" are running this baby a whole new way.

PAUL

(Points to a chair at the table beside him, but Logan stays in place) You're saying you're scared?

LOGAN

(Nods) You ashamed?

PAUL

(Thinks, takes a long swallow from his glass) I guess shame has got very little work from me. *(Faces Logan)* No, I just don't want you boarding a troopship with anything less than a full deck of cards. *(Smiles)* You may need your aces.

LOGAN

That's what *I'm* saying, Dad.

PAUL

Stop wanting them then.

LOGAN

Sir?

PAUL

Stop giving a damn.

LOGAN

I'll be dead on the beach.

PAUL

You'd be happy though.

LOGAN

Great Jesus, Dad!

PAUL

(Grips his glass and stares at the half-inch of bourbon) Have I had too much? I still can't believe you aren't just off on a Boy Scout trip.

LOGAN

(Nods) It changes now.

PAUL

A lot does, I guess. *(Looks slowly round the room)*

LOGAN

You won't move, will you?

PAUL

This is too much house.

LOGAN

Tee can handle it all. She always has. I doubt Mother ever cooked twenty-five meals.

PAUL

(Grins) She made really good cheese sandwiches when I first met her—trimmed off the crusts and fried them in butter. Then she found Tee to help her. Tee knew so much more. Will she be here tomorrow?

LOGAN

Every morning you want her, till Judgment Day.

PAUL

I'll rattle at *night. (Looks straight at Logan)* You won't ever live here again, do you think?

LOGAN

(Picks up a cloth potholder from the counter, studies it a moment—his mother's embroidery) I really can't say.

PAUL

You'll want to finish college—so Christmas and Easter for two more years, you'd call on me here. Then you'd be turning out money and babies somewhere up the line where people want to be. Nobody your age, after hearing this war, will ever want to live in this much peace again.

LOGAN

(Seems to nod, replaces the potholder, takes up his glass, walks to the table and sits five feet from his father's right hand) Just keep the piano. If I return victorious from Mount Fujiyama, I may want to sit here and play for six months.

PAUL

(Smiles) I'll keep it tuned and ready.

LOGAN

Then I'll try to be something—a lawyer, I guess.

PAUL

Well, hurry. Your father may need your help.

LOGAN

(Studies him quickly, decides he's joking) Hold your horses another few years. Then I'll give you cut rates on a first-class defense.

Paul smiles, then stares at his glass in sudden gravity.

LOGAN

How will you be?

Paul seems not to hear.

LOGAN

Dad, what'll you do?

Paul continues staring down but stretches his right hand out toward Logan and, using his thumb and little finger, walks the hand in quick comic circles; then collapses it, exhausted.

Logan laughs and leans to pat the hand in mock consolation.

LOGAN

You entering the postwar Olympics?

PAUL

Just the Great Race of Life—the distance event. Selling pianos and a few church organs through the countryside, deprived as it is. *(Drinks a swallow)* If they still *make* pianos.

LOGAN

Sure they will—

PAUL

They will but will anybody play them again? Won't everybody be out riding like cyclones?

LOGAN

For what?

PAUL

(Faces Logan, eyes shining) Hell, for *joy!* This country's promised *joy*. Now people mean to find it.

LOGAN

Let them. They'll have to stop eventually.

PAUL

—In the ground, when they've burrowed six feet underground.

LOGAN

You've done a lot of riding.

PAUL

Worn myself out.

LOGAN

I always told myself you were happy. When I'd walk in from a really big day in the fourth damn grade and Mother and Tee would be sitting right here, both blue as ink, I'd tell myself "There is one person out there, happy as me; and he'll be back Friday evening by six."

PAUL

(Calmer) What made you think that?

LOGAN

(Thinks) The way you'd meet me. You could sell pianos—or not sell a one—from Monday through Friday on the sizzling roads and still look glad to see a normal child.

PAUL

That's no big virtue.

LOGAN

Mother asked you once "Who is this tired stranger?" You said "The truest heart south of Baltimore" and she said "Welcome!"

PAUL

(Smiles) She did what she could. *(Empties his glass in another long swallow)* You coming with me?

LOGAN

Sir?

PAUL

Tomorrow—I've got to sell *something* this week. Little two-day trip. You've plumbed Idaho. Now learn the mysteries of eastern Carolina.

LOGAN

I may not need another mystery this week.

PAUL

(Thinks, then calmly) Just people—having daily lives—nothing too strange.

LOGAN

It's not too soon?

PAUL

For what?

LOGAN

Leaving here, right after a funeral.

PAUL

Let me guarantee this much—we'll miss her all our lives, and what any damned bystander has to say means as much as cold spit.

LOGAN

(Nods) What time?

6

The next morning, eight o'clock.

Logan opens the front door and steps onto the porch, his shaving kit in hand.

Paul is dimly seen in the hall, speaking to Tee.

PAUL

—Tomorrow evening probably, by suppertime. Have something good ready.

TEE

Have I ever cooked bad?

Paul sees the funeral flowers on the door—a spray of white with palm-leaf trimmings. He thinks a moment, then sets down his well-used Gladstone bag and carefully lifts the flowers from their nail.

PAUL

(Holding them out) You want these, Tee?

TEE

(Shaking her head) Bad luck and you know it.

PAUL

(Smells them slowly, then thrusts them on Tee) Burn them please. Right now.

7

Three hours later, fifty miles east. A small-town furniture store with three pianos against the back wall.

Paul and Logan are beside the pianos, talking with the manager—Mr. Applegate.

PAUL

(Stroking the lid of a dark upright) We're having a hell of a time with wood—had a whole boatload of mahogany sunk by one torpedo two weeks ago—but I think I can promise you three more uprights and one or two spinets between now and Christmas.

APPLEGATE

Who's going to play them, Paul? There're not enough children round here now to field a team, much less play scales.

PAUL

They'll be back any day. This war's bound to end; and then broad droves of the horniest boys since Greece took Troy will be landing here, pumping out children like rivets and signing them up for piano lessons.

APPLEGATE

I wish I could believe you.

PAUL

(Looking round for Logan, who is raising the lid on the sole baby grand) There's your proof—my boy there, aching for a chance.

APPLEGATE

(To Logan, joking) I heard they kept you boys supplied with girls, whole tentfuls of ready girls every weekend.

LOGAN

(Nods, straight-faced) Yes sir, they do—no extra charge. No music though. It's music we're *craving.*

Logan strikes two chords in heraldry, Da-Dum. Then not sitting down, he starts a slow boogie—elegant and perfect. After ten seconds he breaks off mid-bar, turns and bows to Applegate.

LOGAN

(Mock serious still) That's all we boys are fighting for.

APPLEGATE

(Laughs, claps his hands lightly, then turns to Paul) Send me two uprights.

PAUL

And one more spinet?

APPLEGATE

All right.

Paul bows toward Logan and all three laugh.

8

An hour later, off the main road east. Warm noon sun.

Paul and Logan have stopped by an old bridge across a small river to eat the lunch Tee packed for them. They sit on the ground on a blanket by the car at the foot of an oak. They have finished the food and are resting now, on their backs looking up.

PAUL

(Quietly) It seems like we did this before.

LOGAN

Sir? Did what?

PAUL

Lay back like this—here—years ago. You were out of school—fourth or fifth grade—and were traveling with me. We stopped here—trees were green—it was hot—you were swimming back-stroke.

LOGAN

(Turns to see his father, who does not meet the gaze) No sir. Not me. I wish it had been.

PAUL

Your mother was always saying you'd be bored, and I gave in to her.

LOGAN

Maybe she was right but I'm sorry she won—she won a lot, didn't she? Anyhow, I used to stay home and think about you. I didn't exactly have a life myself—just other dumb kids and books to read—so I spent a lot of time making up lives for you.

PAUL

(Laughs lightly, then turns to look once quickly) What were they like?

LOGAN

(Sits up and faces the river) What you did when you were gone, what you turned into. See, I had to convince myself you didn't just vanish every week when you left me and Mother.

PAUL

Maybe I did.

LOGAN

No, you turned *into* things.

PAUL

(Smiles, looking up) Yeah, a hot tired piano salesman, eating pig scraps at crossroad cafés.

LOGAN

A lot more than that.

PAUL

(Rising on his elbows and searching Logan's face) Want to tell me what else?

LOGAN

Everything I was scared of—you kidnaped children and were

drunk every night: you danced in roadhouses and let women follow you back to cool rooms in dark tourist courts where nobody knew your name.

PAUL

(Laughs) How much did that worry you?

LOGAN

Not a bit. It just made me hope for you even harder.

PAUL

(Lying back again) When was all this?

LOGAN

Oh, till I was fourteen and had my own secrets.

PAUL

Did you ever tell your mother?

LOGAN

Not a syllable, no. That was my other job—not bothering her.

PAUL

Where did *she* think I was?

LOGAN

(Studying Paul a moment) Where you said you'd be, I guess—in country hotel rooms with one rusty fan and no telephone, reading *True Detective Stories* half the night.

PAUL

Did she have a good time?

LOGAN

When?—thinking of you?

PAUL

In her life—the years you watched her life.

LOGAN

I never much thought so till I hit the army. Not that she seemed like any big tragedy; but blue too much of the time—all the memories she staged on all the anniversaries: her father's stroke, her brother losing half his leg in France on November

10th, 1918. She had a big stock. I'd avoid her those days; but once I hit the army and heard how bad everybody else's mother had been *every day*, then I realized mine had been easy on me.

PAUL

You were good to her.

LOGAN

Everybody else was. She never harmed a soul.

PAUL

Something harmed her though, long before I knew her. Something crushed a part of her that grown people need.

LOGAN

What?

PAUL

(Thinks) A hoper, I guess. She lacked normal hopes. She expected the worst, doubted every good moment.

LOGAN

She was right after all. The worst hit her, broadside.

PAUL

(Sits up carefully, looks at his shoes, then faces Logan gravely) That may need explaining.

LOGAN

(Mildly puzzled) Dad, she *died*—young as you, four days ago, neither one of us there. *(By the end he is visibly moved)*

PAUL

(Calm) Tee was with her. Tee held her. Tee said your mother knew her.

LOGAN

(Quiet but firm) That was not good enough.

PAUL

Nothing ever was or will be.

Logan is increasingly moved and angered. He stands and takes two steps toward the river. When he's calmed a little, he speaks toward the water.

LOGAN

Is that the absolute best you've got to raise the spirits of a poor soldier-boy bound to liberate Asia?

Paul thinks, then stands, removes his jacket and rolls his sleeves to the elbows neatly.

Logan turns in the silence and watches, baffled.

Paul smiles to Logan but walks forward past him, squats and carefully washes his hands in the river shallows. His hands still submerged, Paul looks up to Logan.

PAUL

You ready?

LOGAN

For what?

PAUL

You asked for raised spirits.

Logan does not understand but removes his jacket, squats by Paul and sinks his own hands in water surprisingly warm for March.

LOGAN

What warmed it so early?

PAUL

My smoldering heart— *(Smiles to Logan)*

Logan faces him gravely.

Paul stirs his right hand, then accurately scoops a full palm of water onto Logan's face.

Logan rises, laughing and brushing himself.

9

Two hours later, three o'clock, they have pushed on east into flat farmland and tall pinewoods.

Their car (Logan driving now) threads the main street of a village—six or seven store buildings, a filling station. The street is empty till they reach the end of buildings.

There two older men are standing at the edge of pavement, talking (one white, one black). They watch as the car nears; and when they see Paul, the black man raises a hand in silent greeting.

Paul turns and smiles in response.

LOGAN

He own a piano?

PAUL

He's the bootlegger, no.

LOGAN

Should we patronize him?

PAUL

(Points forward) I think I can cover our needs. If not, I know his house.

LOGAN

(Looks round, incredulous) We staying *here* tonight?

PAUL

(Points left for a turn) We may, we may.

They are now at the absolute end of the town—a few houses to their left, fields to their right.

LOGAN

We sleeping in the fields?

PAUL

(Smiles) Hold your horses. *(Points another turn left)*

A two-story schoolhouse, a dirt parking lot with three or four cars. Logan turns in.

PAUL

Now stop. *(As they park he studies Logan's profile)* We made it.

LOGAN

To where?

10

Five minutes later in the big dim hallway of the school, Paul stops at a shut door. Logan is behind him.

The voices of children singing leak through—the Czarist National Hymn of Russia.

Logan is about to ask a puzzled question.

Paul silences him with a finger held to his own mouth, then opens the door enough to see a woman leading the chorus toward a close.

The children—eleven and twelve years old (all white)—see Paul first but sing on.

Then the woman—Lena Brock—senses a presence and looks over quickly. She smiles slightly, goes on conducting with her left hand and comes to the door to usher Paul in. She is thirty-eight, still winsome with an undemonstrative force.

Logan follows, unexpected.

Lena smiles but barely conceals her surprise at Logan's entry.

Paul goes to a side wall and stands as if accustomed to being there.

Logan follows uneasily.

Lena moves toward a small piano at the front of the room (one of Paul's spinets) and stands there, waving the hymn to its ending.

LENA

Beautiful, children—the National Hymn of Russia, our

strongest ally. And you sang it with no piano at all. What is that called, Dayton?

DAYTON

(A boy toward the back of the room) Hard, I guess.

General laughter, a scattered show of hands.

LENA

Adele?

ADELE

A cappella, you said.

LENA

And I told you the truth! *(Laughs)*

The end-of-day bell rings loudly in the hall. A few boys rise.

LENA

Don't forget what I said—listen to the news tonight and copy down any big Russian victories. Then we'll learn the *Polish* anthem. Go quietly now.

The children leave in their best semblance of order, a suppressed melee.

As the last two boys approach Logan at the wall, the Taller Boy seizes Dayton by the hair and pulls his head back.

Dayton howls but slips free and stops before Logan.

DAYTON

(Points to Logan's insignia) Can I have your badge?

LENA

Dayton, that's enough—

LOGAN

They'd arrest me without it.

DAYTON

My brother gave me his. *He's* still running loose.

Logan laughs, unfastens a small enameled shield and hands it to Dayton.

Dayton studies it a moment, then runs to the door where the Taller Boy waits.

LENA

Dayton, you forgot.

TALLER BOY

(Pokes Dayton on the shoulder) Tell him "Thank you," Little Dummy.

DAYTON

I'll make my sister pray for you.

The two boys leave.

LOGAN

(To their backs) Tell her "Quick and don't stop." *(Manages a smile)*

LENA

You should meet his sister. She can half-raise the dead!

A silent moment while the meaning of that settles round the three faces.

PAUL

This is my son, Mrs. Brock.

LENA

—Logan. *(Stays in place behind the piano, not stern but not smiling)*

LOGAN

Yes ma'm. I liked the song.

LENA

Joe Stalin wouldn't. It's the old Czar's anthem. Our music books are ancient, but I haven't told the children.

PAUL

Don't confuse them.

LENA

(Still to Logan) I want them to learn all the allied anthems.

LOGAN

You just teach music?

LENA

Oh no, everything but auto repair. What you need to learn?

LOGAN

(Embarrassed) It'd take all day.

LENA

School's out. I'm free. *(But looks to Paul)*

PAUL

How's the new piano?

LENA

(Patting the lid) Too good for me. *(Steps round, plays a few chords)* One or two bass notes have slipped a little maybe. *(Strikes the notes, slightly sour)* But the children never need them.

PAUL

Those boys' voices will be deepening any day. I'll tune it tomorrow morning early.

Lena nods, then looks a little shyly toward Logan.

LENA

I know *you* play.

LOGAN

(Mildly puzzled at her knowledge) I'm rusty now.

PAUL

Let her hear you.

LOGAN

(Firmly to Paul) Not now.

For a moment they face each other, debating the need for a wrangle.

Lena rises from the bench.

Paul relents and turns to her.

PAUL

We'll take you home.

LENA

Maybe I should work awhile. *(Gestures to a desk and stacks of student papers)*

PAUL

The one thing children have to do is *wait.*

LENA

(Thinks, smiles, begins to gather books) You may still have a lot to learn about children.

PAUL

(Nods) I'm ready.

When Lena is ready, she walks past Paul and stops in front of Logan.

LENA

I'm sorry—

LOGAN

Did you know her?

LENA

(Shakes her head, waits) You any kind of farmer?

LOGAN

I worked Mother's garden.

LENA

She like strawberries?

LOGAN

No. She had them for us though—my father and me.

LENA

Then maybe you're my rescue. I've had berry plants for two weeks now, hoping some wise hand would come help me set them.

LOGAN

(Guarded) Just in sun—full sun, if you've got it.

LENA

(Searches his eyes, then nods) We've got it.

Lena leaves, not looking back to Paul.

Logan shrugs, still puzzled, but follows her.

Paul turns out the light as he leaves last.

They walk in Indian file up the empty hall, past plaster casts of the Venus de Milo and the Winged Victory.

11

Half an hour later, the porch of Lena's house.

Paul is seated in a rocker.

Logan stands at the bottom of the steps in the yard, looking toward the road.

Lena enters from within through the front screen door with a tray of Coca-Colas and glasses.

Paul takes one bottle (no glass).

Lena looks toward Logan's back.

Logan does not turn.

PAUL

Son—

LOGAN

Sir?

PAUL

Sit down and drink this dope—cool and soothing.

Logan stays in place. So Lena takes two steps forward to serve him.

PAUL

(Stops her with a gesture, then stronger to Logan) You've got the whole rest of your life to stand up in. *(Points to an empty rocker beside him)*

LOGAN

(Thinks a moment, looking straight at Paul) That may just be another month at most.

PAUL

(Smiles) Or another five seconds, for all three of us—this *tree* could fall and mash us to jellybeans.

Paul takes a second bottle from Lena's tray and extends it toward Logan.

Logan looks up at the bare tree above them. His self-absorption and vague unease at Lena's presence are yielding now to innate good nature and courtesy. He climbs the steps and accepts the bottle.

LOGAN

(To Lena) Thank you, Mrs. Brock.

LENA

Very welcome, Lieutenant.

A car has stopped in front of the house. A girl steps out and thanks the driver.

The three on the porch all watch in silence as Gail Brock comes toward them through the yard, schoolbooks in her arms. She is fourteen; her all-but womanly face still wears a child's serenity.

Logan is clearly impressed by her beauty and watches her closely.

At the foot of the steps, Gail pauses gravely, looking at Lena.

LENA

Big day?

Gail shakes her head No. She has not looked to Logan, and the effort to avoid him is barely visible.

PAUL

You got your hair cut.

GAIL

(Nodding and touching the ends of her hair) My friend Becky did it. I think she messed it up.

LOGAN

Not at all.

LENA

Gail, this is Lieutenant Logan Melton.

GAIL

(Facing him) Hey. *(Climbs the steps, passes them and opens the screen door)*

LENA

You promised you'd help me plant strawberries.

Gail winces but nods and enters the house.

LENA

(To Logan) Where are you stationed now?

LOGAN

Idaho. I'll be shipping out soon—I'm not supposed to say so.

LENA

I won't tell a soul.

LOGAN

Not a *Japanese* soul. *(Loosens his tie, pulls it off, unbuttons his collar)*

PAUL

There's a minimum of them in rural Carolina.

LENA

I'll just go check on Gail—

LOGAN

Can I help her?

LENA

(Grins) She's changing into work clothes. She'll manage O.K.

LOGAN

With the planting, I mean—you mentioned strawberries. *(Looks to Paul)* We pausing here awhile?

PAUL

(Nods) A while.

LOGAN

We could do it—Gail and I. It wouldn't take long.

LENA

Then I'm sure she'd welcome help. *(Waits, then half-whispers to Logan)* She'd be too proud to ask, but she's always hoped to meet you.

12

Twenty minutes later, four-thirty p.m.

Gail and Logan are squatting in a garden behind the house, planting strawberries with rusty trowels. Gail wears a simple housedress. Logan wears his undershirt and the trousers of his uniform.

Logan faces Gail, who works intently.

They are silent at first.

GAIL

(Not looking up) Don't let Remus bite you.

LOGAN

Who?

GAIL

The snake that lives here. Black as old Uncle Remus.

LOGAN

Too early for snakes. Anyhow, a black snake's the least of my worries.

They work another long silent moment.

Then Logan looks to Gail. His strong response to her open beauty is hindered by thoughts of his likely future.

GAIL

What would be the *most* of your worries?

LOGAN

(Thinks) —Ending the war.

GAIL

You'll have a lot of help. You're not the only soldier.

Logan pauses, then laughs.

GAIL

(Looking up) Are you?

LOGAN

No, there's several million more. They kill us one at a time, just the same.

GAIL

(Pauses, looking round toward the distant woods) Seems pretty safe to me.

LOGAN

I'll be leaving here. *(In all that follows, his vulnerability to Gail's magnetism is shown in small helpless gestures of attraction—any move that will bring his hands nearer to her)*

GAIL

That wouldn't worry *me.*

LOGAN

You been here all your life?

GAIL

More than fourteen years. We moved here right after my father died—I was six months old. My mother had to work, and she only knew music, so she got a job here. They're crazy for music. *(Waits)* I wish it could have been in a lot bigger place.

LOGAN

(Looks round) Seems big enough here—plenty air, plenty trees.

GAIL

(Smiles) Trees mostly don't talk.

LOGAN

What you want to talk about?

GAIL

Just *talk*, to hear myself. Mother's always too tired. Everybody else is children.

LOGAN

Dive in. I'm grown and I'm not a bit tired.

GAIL

How old are you?

LOGAN

Twenty.

GAIL

(Kneels in the row of plants and faces Logan) Does it ever get better?

LOGAN

(Kneeling also) What?

GAIL

I don't know—*life*.

LOGAN

What's wrong with life?

GAIL

(Thinks) Oh, it's *taking* too long.

LOGAN

(Laughs) What you want it to do?

GAIL

Make me grown up—soon.

LOGAN

(Studies her a moment) You're what?—fifteen? You're moving right along.

GAIL

(Unselfconsciously runs a hand across her breasts, half-whispering) Claudia Spencer, one grade ahead of me, is pretty sure she's pregnant.

LOGAN

That's life—speeding up. Where'd she find a father? All boys are in the army.

GAIL

That's what *you* think. We've got plenty boys. I wish they'd draft them sooner.

LOGAN

Don't wish that on anybody, Gail.

GAIL

It's doing *you* good.

LOGAN

(Laughs) How's that?

GAIL

You've grown on up. You look a lot better.

LOGAN

Thank you, I guess. But where've you seen me?

GAIL

(Points quickly to the house) Your father—pictures of you—he's shown us your pictures long as I remember.

LOGAN

Have you known him that long?

GAIL

(Nods) Longer.

LOGAN

(Mildly curious) He's worked with your mother.

GAIL

(Nods, returns to planting) We heard about *your* mother.

LOGAN

How well did you know her?

GAIL

We never saw her.

Logan's initial sense, in the schoolroom, of something strange begins to deepen now.

But Gail, still planting, forestalls him innocently.

GAIL

You haven't even planted enough to earn your supper.

LOGAN

(Returning to work) Are we eating here?

GAIL

(Nods) Are you married?

LOGAN

I thought you knew about me.

GAIL

Not much—just your face.

LOGAN

No ma'm. I'm single. I'll wait to get free. Then I have to finish college.

GAIL

Are you lonesome?

LOGAN

(Laughs and stops again, facing Gail) Not now—not this minute.

Gail looks up, smiles quickly but points him to work again. Soon she turns her back and moves away to another row. When she's worked there a moment, she speaks without looking.

GAIL

If second cousins marry each other, what happens?

LOGAN

(Laughs) Beg your pardon?

GAIL

You know—do they have two-headed babies?

LOGAN

I haven't tried it yet. But there's no big shortage of strangers to love.

GAIL

In the army?

LOGAN

—Army *towns.* And in the whole world.

GAIL

(Thinks) That's why I want to get out of this place.

LOGAN

You in love with your cousin?

Gail turns back to study him carefully, her face entirely neutral.

GAIL

I could probably love you.

LOGAN

(Touched, almost shaken) Not now. I may not last.

GAIL

We're just second cousins—maybe even third.

LOGAN

(Puzzled but still in the grip of her offer) We're no kin at all, to the best of my knowledge.

Gail shakes her head No.

Logan slowly stands.

Gail stays in place, a plant in her hand.

He begins to move toward her.

When he's four steps away, Gail looks back quickly to the distant house—no one in sight. Then she rises to meet him.

Logan's hands stay down; but he pauses a moment, looking past her (though not to the house).

Then he leans to kiss the crown of her head.

Gail accepts that, unmoving.

Logan takes a step backward.

Gail studies him, then closes the gap and cranes up to meet his lips—long but cool.

His hands have stayed down.

Gail steps back and bends to collect her trowel.

Logan does the same.

They rise together.

GAIL

What happens if cousins *kiss*?

LOGAN

Big babies in loud colors—red, green, orange—that come out talking and can sing on-key.

GAIL

(Thinks, then sings softly)

"Over hill, over dale,
We have hit the dusty trail,
And those caissons go rolling along.
In and out, hear them shout,
'Counter-march and right about,'
And those caissons go rolling along."

She has hit upon the song of the Field Artillery, and Logan shows some initial resistance; but as she nears the end of the verse and moves toward the house, he falls in beside her and joins the chorus.

LOGAN AND GAIL

"Then it's hi! hi! hee! in the field artillery,
Sound off your numbers loud and strong—One! Two!
Wher'er you go, you will always know
That those caissons are rolling along.
Keep them rolling!
And those caissons go rolling along."

13

Two minutes later, nearly five o'clock, the kitchen of the house.

Lena is working at the sink.

Paul has removed his tie and is sitting at the central table, calmly reading a magazine.

Soft music comes from a big old radio in a corner and continues throughout. The sense is one of accustomed ease.

Laughter from the back porch steps, climbing feet.

Gail enters briskly with Logan behind her, a little abashed.

PAUL

Sounded like maneuvers out there. Did you finish?

Gail nods and goes to the sink to wash her hands.

Logan brushes his hands together, dusting them off.

LOGAN

(To Lena) They should do all right—course you'll have to wait for berries.

LENA

Thank you, Logan. Thank you very much.

PAUL

She can *not* wait. She's made a walnut pie.

GAIL

I hate black walnuts.

LENA

Then that makes you special.

PAUL

I'm normal. I eat them every chance I get. Logan eats them in his sleep.

LOGAN

(Confused by the air of ease, to Paul) Are you eating here?

Paul frowns at the rudeness.

Gail has watched from the sink. She nods to Logan gravely.

Lena faces Logan.

LENA

You'd both be welcome, Logan, to what we've got.

Logan balks a moment, looks to Gail's back (she is still unsmiling), then again to Paul.

Paul is silent and blank.

GAIL

Guess what we haven't got?

All face her, relieved.

PAUL

What?

GAIL

Whipping cream.

Lena rushes to the refrigerator and looks.

LENA

How did you know that?

GAIL

(Still not turning) I *know* things, Mother. *(Turns quickly to Logan)* I can't eat walnut pie without whipped cream.

PAUL

(Standing, to Gail) Then guide me to cream. We'll go buy some cream.

LENA

(Glancing at the clock) But hurry—just a pint—and smell it for onions.

Gail dries her hands to go.

Logan still stands, confused—is he going with them?

PAUL

You stay here, Son. Try to help out.

LENA

(To Logan) I'll manage. Get some air.

PAUL

He's had air today and plenty more to come. *(To Logan)* Rest here. Ten minutes. Go count Lena's chickens.

Gail is already out of the room.

Paul follows to the door.

PAUL

What else besides cream?

LENA

That's it.

PAUL

Gas is rationed—

LENA

(Smiles) I'm sure.

PAUL

(Going, to Logan) Count the chickens. Kill any snake you see.

The front screen door slams shut.

Logan is still near the kitchen door, standing abandoned and awkward now.

Lena returns to work at the sink.

LENA

There aren't any chickens, Logan. Rest yourself.

LOGAN

(Moving toward a chair at the table) Thank you, ma'm.

LENA

The front room might be a little more peaceful. There *is* a piano. Play me something.

LOGAN

(Standing behind the chair) It's all right here, if I won't bother you.

LENA

I'm *easy* not to bother. *(But she works intently)*

Logan sits slowly and holds upright a moment. Then he bends to rest his head on the table, his eyes on Lena.

In the silence Lena turns to look.

LOGAN

I can't remember the last time I rested.

LENA

Rest is one thing we've got.

Logan shuts his eyes and quickly seems asleep.

Lena turns back to work.

The radio produces an upbeat song.

Logan's eyes reopen but his head stays down.

LOGAN

Maybe I've been too far for my age. *(Smiles crookedly)*

LENA

You've seen a lot of places.

LOGAN

(Still down) I've seen a lot of trains—the insides of trains from here to Idaho, the old airplane that brought me home.

LENA

I'd love to fly.

LOGAN

No you wouldn't, no ma'm.

LENA

Not now. After all this mess is over.

LOGAN

(Suddenly sits up) You think it *will* be?

LENA

Sure—before another Christmas.

LOGAN

Will I live to see it?

LENA

(Forced to turn and see him) Christmas or peace?

LOGAN

I'd take either one.

LENA

You look strong to me.

LOGAN

My mother *looked* strong.

Lena pauses and then turns back to work.

LOGAN

What kin are you to her?

LENA

(Waits) I never got to see her.

LOGAN

Gail said we were cousins. Mother had a world of cousins—I barely knew five.

LENA

Gail thinks a lot. Remember when you were fourteen years old.

LOGAN

I'm thinking right now.

LENA

(Looks back quickly, smiling) You were told to rest.

LOGAN

(Gentle but firm) I've been told everything but what I need.

LENA

That's a normal predicament, wouldn't you say?

LOGAN

(Still gently but strengthening) What?—have your young mother fall dead on the floor a few days before you're due to ship out to face a billion armed Japanese defending their homes, and me in just *skin? (Touches his cheek)*

LENA

(Calmly) I said you'd make it.

LOGAN

You said I was strong. I'm not—the world knows it.

Logan's face is suddenly bathed in tears. He stares on at Lena, unashamed or desperate.

In the silence she turns and receives the sight. She stays in place a moment, then dries her hands, steps to the table and sits facing Logan. Her hands are on the edge but do not reach toward him.

By now, real pain contorts his tears—the shame of fear and the shame of pent-up grief for his mother.

LENA

(Half-whispers) Nobody's here but me, and I don't count. Let it all out, as much as will come.

LOGAN

(After long silence, shakes his head; then with great difficulty) This is not for me.

LENA

I think I know that.

LOGAN

(Still straining) I loved my mother more than anything else.

LENA

She wanted you to.

LOGAN

I caused her to die.

LENA

You were two thousand miles away.

LOGAN

It worried her to death—me going to war. She had plans for me. They were getting all ruined.

LENA

(Smiling) They're not. You look fine to me. You're safe.

LOGAN

I *may* be—I may turn out to be an honorable man with good work to do and strong happy children. She didn't wait to see.

LENA

It was just her time. I *believe* in fate—I've had to. If I didn't, I'd have run wild years ago—the stuff I've seen. *(But she smiles again)*

LOGAN

(Studies her—the first time) Who are you?

LENA

(Waits, gestures round her) What you see.

Logan looks round as though there were answers to find.

LOGAN

Why am I here?

LENA

(Thinks, then laughs and stands) To try my grand food—I cook much better than I teach children music. You're bound to be hungry.

LOGAN

(Also stands) I don't think so—

His grief, fear and bafflement are at their strongest. He walks to the open kitchen door, steps out, takes the back steps quickly, then runs through the yard toward the garden and the woods.

Lena pauses, then slowly walks to the door and sees him vanish in the darkening trees.

14

Immediately after, five-thirty.

Paul and Gail are returning in the car, with a small bag of groceries. They ride in easy silence, their faces dazed by private thoughts. At last, almost in sight of Lena's—

PAUL

Did he measure up?

GAIL

Sir?—to what?

PAUL

Logan—did he meet your expectations?

GAIL

(Thinks) I guess so. *(Turns to her window, a stretch of trees)* I'd waited so long, I thought he'd seem older.

PAUL

He's tired today.

GAIL

Of what?

PAUL

This war.

GAIL

I'm tired of the war. It's all I remember—Franklin D. Roosevelt and rationed shoes.

PAUL

You need new shoes?

GAIL

Not really—maybe sandals if summer ever comes.

PAUL

We'll see to that. *(Long pause)* Has your mother been O.K.?

GAIL

(Still staring aside) You saw her. You've known her much longer.

PAUL

Pardon me.

GAIL

(Waits a long silence, then faces his profile) Are *you* all right?

PAUL

(Smiles) I haven't checked lately. *(Feels his heart)* The *clock* is still ticking.

GAIL

Was the funeral nice?

PAUL

(Thinks, then smiles) Nice, very nice. Even *she'd* have been pleased. Mostly music. I throttled the minister.

GAIL

Really?

PAUL

I told him any *words* might be hard on Logan, having come so far and facing his future.

GAIL

(Waits, then with unexpected fervor) I love him.

PAUL

Not yet.

GAIL

That's what Logan said. I can disobey you both.

They stare forward at the road in silence.

15

Immediately after.

Logan is walking in a slow intensity, on a path through the woods behind Lena's house. Sooner than he expects, he breaks through onto a clearing—a small creek, late sun. He turns to follow the water downstream and, round a bend, comes on a ring of stones laid out on the bank—a once-cleared space returning to weeds—ten feet across with a big flat central stone.

He enters, studies the ground, sees something, bends, scratches at it. First he unearths the arm of a small doll. Then he digs on, finds the rest and lifts it—remains of a doll ten inches long, missing one eye and badly weathered but grinning gamely. He replaces it, covers it carefully, presses the dirt with his foot.

Then he sits on the central stone and stares up at the sky through branches.

16

Immediately after.

Lena is setting four places at the table in her dining room. She pauses to hear Paul's car arrive but continues working as Paul and Gail enter.

Gail goes to her own room.

Paul goes to the kitchen, finds it empty.

PAUL

(Setting a bag on the counter) Anybody home?

LENA

(Long pause) No.

Paul follows her voice, finds her standing on the far side of the dining table—finished and facing him.

PAUL

You are, plain as day.

LENA

But you said *home*. Whose home is this?

Paul winces slightly, then shakes his head—she is talking too openly, too soon.

LENA

(Calm) He's gone.

PAUL

Logan? Where?

LENA

I don't know—out the back.

PAUL

I didn't think you'd tell him.

LENA

You did, Paul—you know it. You hoped you could leave here to buy a pint of cream and come back ten minutes later—all fixed, seventeen years dissolved: one big *family*, happy as frogs.

PAUL

Are frogs happy?—no, maybe you're right. Sure I wanted no pain for everybody here. Wouldn't that be normal?—they're all I've got.

LENA

(Thinks, nods) That would be normal—for you, Paul. For you.

She walks directly past him toward the kitchen.

Paul stands a moment, then steps to the neat table, strokes a bare plate with his fingers. Then he follows Lena.

But the kitchen is empty again.

PAUL

Lena?

LENA

(Long pause) I'm on the back steps.

PAUL

(Looking to the pantry) You want a short drink?

LENA

No, I don't.

Paul goes to the pantry, finds the fifth of bourbon behind rows of food, returns to the sink, pours himself four ounces straight and knocks it back in one long swallow. He shudders hard, then turns toward the front of the house.

PAUL

Gail?

GAIL

(Distant, muffled) What?

PAUL

Don't call me *what*. Where are you?

GAIL

Getting dressed.

PAUL

You were already dressed.

GAIL

I'll be there in a minute.

PAUL

(Looking toward Lena) Take your time. We're dying, is all—slow starvation.

He pours another drink (two ounces) and swallows. Then he goes to Lena; stands a moment, looking out toward the dimming woods, and sits two steps above her.

PAUL

You given up cooking?

LENA

(Not turning) It's in the oven, ready whenever you are.

PAUL

I'm ready. Gail's beautifying herself for Logan. He'll be back soon.

LENA

What makes you think so?

PAUL

I've known him all his life.

LENA

He hasn't known you.

PAUL

Well, you seem to have helped him. He'll be in soon.

LENA

I can teach little children to halfway sing. I don't offer courses in the mysteries of God.

PAUL

(Smiling) Am I one of those?

LENA

You're right up there with earthquakes, glaciers—trench mouth. *(Turns back to face him, almost smiles)* I didn't tell Logan a thing, Paul—really. That's your choice to make. Gail seems to have told him they were some kind of cousins, her and him.

PAUL

She's fallen for him.

LENA

(Looking outward again) I did too, seventeen years ago.

PAUL

He was three years old. You didn't *know* about him.

LENA

I met you—I knew you—he's almost the image of you at that age, every way *I* can see.

PAUL

He's nicer than me—he pays more attention. So he has more worries. When I met you I didn't have a care to my name. *(Lays both hands on Lena's shoulders)*

LENA

(Looking outward) The whole Depression was one year away. You had a wife that you said barely noticed you.

PAUL

Don't blame her now. She was tending Logan. I doubt a woman ever loved a child more than she loved Logan back then. I was just a trusty friend that showed up for weekends.

LENA

(His hands on her still, still looking out) I haven't told Logan a single secret, Paul.

PAUL

What drove him off then?

LENA

We mentioned his mother—and the war—and her worrying. He *knows* she died of dread for him. So now he plans to die just to even the score.

PAUL

(Takes his hands back) He very well might.

Lena turns half-around and studies Paul a moment.

He waits, then nods.

LENA

Then go find him now.

PAUL

And tell him what?

LENA

(Thinks) —That he's welcome here. Anything else you want, just no more lies.

Paul thinks, nods, studies Lena. Then he bends to kiss her.

She accepts him calmly.

The sound of steps behind them. They continue close—Paul's chin on the crown of Lena's hair, both looking to the woods.

Gail is just above them, dressed and combed. She takes the sight of the adults in stride.

GAIL

Where's Logan?

PAUL

On a hike.

GAIL

Does he have to practice?

PAUL

Oh yes. They give you leave, but you got to practice.

LENA

(Points) He's down by the creek, I guess. He *headed* there.

GAIL

Is he coming in to eat?

PAUL

I'll go get him.

GAIL

Let me.

PAUL

(Rising) Help your mother.

GAIL

I know the woods best.

PAUL

(Facing her firmly) No. I said I was going and I am. I'll find him. You wait.

Paul descends the steps and moves through the yard, pausing to check a parked lawnmower.

Dusky light. Lena sits on.

Gail slowly sits in Paul's place.

They face the woods, silent.

17

Six o'clock.

Paul reaches the bank of the creek without calling. He pauses there a moment and stares upstream. The light is dimmer. He turns downstream and, every few steps, calls at normal volume—

PAUL

Logan—

No answer.

As Paul flanks the abandoned ring of stones, he fails to see Logan, who is lying on his back with his head on the central stone, his feet toward Paul.

Logan's eyes are barely open and register no recognition of his father.

When Paul has walked well past and called again, Logan answers.

LOGAN

(Still supine) He's here.

Paul walks toward the voice but takes awhile to find him. At last, in the entrance to the ring, Paul stops.

PAUL

How is he?

LOGAN

Haven't asked him lately.

PAUL

(Enters and sits on a flat stone) He'd better check soon. This ground looks damp. *(Lays his palm on the ground)* He'll be rusting out fast.

LOGAN

Good.

PAUL

(Waits) Sit up, Son. I've lost enough friends.

Logan slowly pulls up, then sits on the stone he has leaned against. The doll he discovered is now at his feet. He bends to touch it.

PAUL

Where'd you rescue that?

LOGAN

In here. It was buried.

PAUL

(Bends to look) Some old friend of Gail's.

LOGAN

What is this place?

PAUL

A creek bank. Some woods.

LOGAN

You could answer me. I'm harmless now.

PAUL

(Smiles) When were you harmful?

LOGAN

Till the day Mother died—I could tell on you.

PAUL

What did you know?

LOGAN

Absolutely nothing.

PAUL

What did you think?

LOGAN

(Lifts the doll to his knees) —That you were several people.

PAUL

Did you like any of them?

LOGAN

The happy one, I told you.

PAUL

(Waits) Thank you. He's still alive, I guess—not as young as he was.

LOGAN

But *happy*, right?

PAUL

I will be again, I trust. We've just had a funeral.

LOGAN

(Calmly) And you may have another one. How would *that* leave you?

PAUL

A good deal sadder. Your mother had a life; you haven't had yours.

LOGAN

Lena Brock says I'll have it. *(Faces Paul)* While you were at the store, she promised me I'd make it.

PAUL

Then you will. She's *smart.*

LOGAN

Who is she?

PAUL

You've seen her—a grade-school teacher with a daughter to raise.

LOGAN

The daughter says we're kin. Gail told me she's my cousin.

PAUL

She's not.

LOGAN

What is she then? What is all this here?

Paul waits, then rises and moves to the old doll lying on the ground. He lifts it by a leg and takes it with him back to his seat. He holds it out before him, studying it.

PAUL

This is a doll I gave Gail Brock for Christmas when she was maybe four years old. *(Touches the doll's empty eye socket)* When it went half-blind, we buried it here and got a new one—a whole string of new ones down through the years till just the other day, seems like, she outgrew them.

Paul rises again and this time returns the doll to its grave. He covers it carefully with dirt, then sits.

LOGAN

Is that my answer?

PAUL

(Waits, then smiles) Ought to be—smart as you are.

LOGAN

She's your daughter.

PAUL

I'm her father.

LOGAN

What's Lena?

PAUL

Her mother—all you saw was true. I never lied to you.

LOGAN

You recall *I* had a mother. How much truth did she see?

PAUL

Don't you think that was her and my business, Son?

LOGAN

Yes sir, I do—long as she was alive to watch it and suffer. But now you've landed me in it, face down.

PAUL

Your mother never watched one second of this, never knew it was here.

LOGAN

She's bound to have felt it. She hardly *had* skin.

PAUL

Did she tell you she did?

LOGAN

She very seldom told me things about you.

PAUL

And she told you everything she felt—*you* were what she felt.

LOGAN

Then why have *you* told me—and now, of all times?

PAUL

I always wanted to tell you somehow. When you'd run out to meet me on Friday evening, it was all I could do not to tell you right then. I wanted you to watch both halves of my contentment and share it if you could. I still do now. You're a full strong man. When I'm gone, you'll need to know.

LOGAN

You're trusting I'll outlast you.

PAUL

You said Lena promised you. Lena's hardly ever wrong.

The light is scarce now.

Logan stands and walks to the doll's covered grave. With one foot he slowly but firmly packs the dirt. Then he looks to Paul and holds his arms out loosely at his sides—a shrug of dazed bafflement.

PAUL

Supper's ready, if you are.

LOGAN

What if I'm not?

PAUL

It's ready all the same. We'd eat it without you—wouldn't relish it much.

LOGAN

I doubt I know enough to walk in there again.

PAUL

I'll tell it all there. I can tell it truer there.

LOGAN

What does Gail know?

PAUL

The bare-bone facts—Lena told her two years ago.

LOGAN

That didn't set her back?

PAUL

Considerably, at first. She wouldn't speak to me for two weeks running, till she saw she didn't have much of a choice—it was speak or go dumb to one of the two things on earth that loved her.

LOGAN

(Nods) She's looking elsewhere.

PAUL

For what?

LOGAN

Things to love her—more men than you.

PAUL

(Thinks, then rises) She'll find them.

LOGAN

She told me we were cousins.

PAUL

She used to believe that. She was sounding you out.

LOGAN

I kissed her.

PAUL

That was typical, at least.

LOGAN

(Half-smiles) Of what?

PAUL

—The *block. (Taps his own chest)* The block you're chipped from, like it or not.

Paul gestures for Logan to precede him out.

Logan stays in place.

LOGAN

I may not like it.

PAUL

I'm what you've got.

LOGAN

I may not want you. *(Walks to the back of the circle and looks toward the house, hid by trees)* I can hitch out of here now, clean as a whistle, and be back in Idaho and never *see* you.

PAUL

I hope you won't.

LOGAN

Why?—to save your face with this other crowd? *(Points toward Lena's)*

PAUL

Not much of a crowd—less if *you* go.

Logan steps outside the stones that edge the ring and moves toward the woods—pathless, nearly dark.

PAUL

I can tell you why.

Logan crashes out of sight through the thicket.

PAUL

(Louder) Show a little mercy—you die, it'll kill me.

Silence from Logan, then a slow crackle in the leaves as he turns. He comes back as far as the edge of the ring and stands, obscured.

LOGAN

You may have earned that.

Paul takes two steps toward him.

Logan takes a step back.

PAUL

(Hotly) Who are you to judge me?

LOGAN

Something you made, that's watched you closely for twenty years now—all you'd let me see. *(Comes two steps forward, his foot on a stone at the edge of the ring)* I dreamed up whole happy lives for you but nothing like this—a small-time cheat.

Paul, for years, has dreaded hearing that. It hits him now like a great body blow. He rides out the first pain, then goes back and sits in his former place.

PAUL

May I speak to that? Then do what you have to.

Logan waits, nods once, but stays in place.

PAUL

I can't talk to somebody staring *down* on me.

Slowly Logan steps back into the ring but sits on the edge. He faces Paul blankly.

PAUL

(Thinks) A *cheat?* Well, O.K. if it makes you feel lighter. But aside from what I told your mother in our wedding vows—and God in Heaven knows *they* can't be kept—I never broke a promise to cherish her.

LOGAN

(Points toward Lena's) This is *cherishing?*

PAUL

(Thinks, nods) Yes. I'm coming to that. But I asked to be heard—listen please or leave.

Logan bends and traces lines in the dirt.

PAUL

—A *cheat:* sure, take it. But small-time, no. I may not be the world's best music salesman—though I think I've brought pleasure to a good many homes—but what you can't see is big, Logan, *big. (Taps his chest again and goes on with real intensity, though with a salesman's practiced fluency and speed)* I've got a lot in here—or they *put* a lot in; it's not my fault. Your mother was a kind intelligent person, and I loved her every day of her life that I knew her. But, Son, she couldn't handle *half* of me.

Logan raises a hand to stop his father.

Paul nods but continues.

PAUL

Before you were born, I'd begun to know that your mother needed much less from life than me. She could sit in a room and watch daylight spread across a plaster wall, millimeters at a time *(Shakes his head in wonder)* and be calm as a leaf. *Saints* do the same thing.

Logan can nod now, yielding slightly.

PAUL

Anyhow, she gave me what she had to give—three days of me a week was plenty for her; she could brace herself for that—and here you came.

LOGAN

—The accident.

PAUL

Not at all. I planned you as carefully as the Normandy invasion. I thought you'd bring her on into the world, get some fresh blood moving my way through her veins—

LOGAN

But she just watched me like daylight on the wall.

PAUL

(Thinks, smiles) Of course, she didn't have to change diapers on daylight—she *worked* on you.

LOGAN

You'd brought her to life.

PAUL

(Thinks) Yes—for you.

LOGAN

Did you blame me for it?

PAUL

(Firmly) Never. Not once.

LOGAN

You'd already found Lena.

PAUL

Not for three years, no—more than one thousand days: lying round country towns in hot rented rooms, hoping some soul would scrape up the money and want a piano. And I didn't *find* Lena, didn't hunt her down. She was just there one day.

LOGAN

Needing a piano—

PAUL

I started that in her, the music part. She was teaching geometry—right out of school herself—and rooming in a house where I used to stay.

LOGAN

Here?

PAUL

Oh no. *(Points)* —In Fulton, deep *down* in the sticks: some boys in her class had sons of their own. It wasn't till I knew she was pregnant that I moved her. She saw I was married, *(Shows his wedding band)* and I saw it wasn't right in any way except the way I needed—*she could use me up.* Whatever else you think, believe one thing—Lena Brock filled every other hunger I had, that you didn't fill. Back then I could watch her—watch her shape in a room—and feel repaid for everything I'd lost.

LOGAN

When did you marry her?

PAUL

(A little surprised) I had a wife, Son—till just the other day.

LOGAN

Who did people think you were?—Lena's family and friends.

PAUL

She'd been raised by an aunt in South Carolina—her parents died young, in the flu epidemic. And once she moved here, she was just a young widow with a baby girl.

LOGAN

(Persisting) Who were you though? Who are you now?

PAUL

I've never asked her. She's made her own arrangements.

LOGAN

How can she be happy?

PAUL

I wouldn't ask her that.

LOGAN

—Thanksgiving, Christmas, Easter: you were always with us. She and Gail got—what?—three nights a week?

PAUL

Less most weeks. I've had to do my job.

LOGAN

How could they stand it?

PAUL

They've got a private strength they've managed to store. *(Waits)* They've wanted to know *you*—

LOGAN

Now you'll bring them home.

PAUL

It's *your* home and *mine.*

LOGAN

Will you move here?

PAUL

(Waits, smiles, then rises) You always want to be a long-range *prophet.* All I can prophesy from here is supper. We're long overdue.

Paul bows slightly at the waist and gestures with a hand toward the exit from the ring.

Logan stays in place, seated, facing his father. His last question survives on his face.

Paul steps toward him, stops an arm's-length away.

PAUL

You're not the only thing here that has to die, Son. Chances are, you'll outlast me by years—me and half of these trees. *(Gestures overhead)* Don't store up memories too hard to bear. *(Extends his right hand and tentatively smiles)* Bless me old prophet.

Logan studies it a moment, then clasps it with his left hand and accepts a pull upward.

LOGAN

What do I say—in there—if I go?

PAUL

Everything your mother taught you—kind courtesy, at least.

Logan faces his father, two feet away. He searches Paul's face and gives no response; but when Paul breaks the gaze and turns to leave, Logan follows him out.

They walk past the creek and into the dark still woods in silence.

18

Five minutes later, Lena's backyard.

Paul moves first from darkness into the porch light's glow.

He stops at the foot of the steps and waits for Logan.

Logan stops three paces back.

The sound of a piano comes from the house—an adequate performance of Chopin's Prelude in D Flat.

LOGAN

Which one is that? *(Nods his head toward the house)*

PAUL

Gail, I guess—she picks the heavy stuff.

LOGAN

Why not call her my sister?

PAUL

(Thinks, unsmiling) That's your choice to make.

LOGAN

I haven't made it yet.

PAUL

(Half-smiles) What you call *me* now?

LOGAN

(Waits) Big Mystery of the Ages—

PAUL

(Laughs) I hope Time has got something bigger to unfold.

LOGAN

(Nods) You mentioned eating supper. That'll do for a start.

Paul nods, turns, climbs the steps with Logan close behind.

The Chopin is ending.

19

Lena's dining room, seven o'clock.

Lena is seated at one end of the table, Paul at the other.

They have finished the main course, and Gail has gone to the kitchen to fetch the walnut pie.

Logan faces her empty chair.

LOGAN

(To Lena) Were there any Russian triumphs?

LENA

(Smiles, puzzled) Beg your pardon?

LOGAN

You told your class to listen to the news.

LENA

Lord, I forgot.

GAIL

(From the kitchen, whipping cream) I didn't. We've captured most of Iwo Jima now.

PAUL

How was Mrs. Roosevelt's day?

LENA

She seems to be standing still for a change. *(Smiles)* Tired as me.

PAUL

She won't rest long. *(To Logan)* You get to Japan, she'll be there to meet you—Eleanor with fresh hot doughnuts on the beach.

The joke falls flat.

Lena glances to Logan.

Logan traces deep lines with a fingernail in the tablecloth.

Gail appears in the door with the pie and a bowl of whipped cream.

LENA

Here's some fresh cream for now.

Gail sets it before her, while Lena brings plates from the side-board. Gail sits and Lena, standing, carefully serves the splendid pie. Logan gets the first plate.

LOGAN

Thank you both.

GAIL

Thank yourself. You earned it.

Logan waits while all the others are served. He is still but not calm—consciously subdued.

Lena sets the remains of the pie on the sideboard and takes her chair again. As she lifts her fork—

LENA

This will have to stand in for champagne. *(Takes a small piece of pie on her fork, holds it out)* —Logan's safe and certain return home soon.

Gail and Paul follow suit.

Logan watches Gail gravely.

GAIL

(Suddenly fervent) Let this be your home now.

Paul glances to Lena.

Lena shows no response but looks to Logan.

Logan takes a slow bite of pie.

LOGAN

(To Gail) You don't know me yet. I'm no sort of hero, in war or peace. *(Thinks, then to Lena)* My mother had me planned as the first big Protestant piano genius with short *combed* hair. *(To*

Paul) I didn't have the patience to work alone. *(To Gail again)* But thank you still.

GAIL

We don't have to *know* you. I told you we'd been looking at pictures of you ever since I remember.

Logan eats another bite.

Paul and Lena are eating watchfully.

LOGAN

(To Gail) I regret you had to put up with that. *(Turns to Lena)* You too, Mrs. Brock.

Gail looks to Lena, then back to Logan.

GAIL

We liked it. Tell him, Mother.

Lena looks to Paul.

Paul nods.

Lena sets down her fork and turns to Logan, unsmiling.

LENA

We knew your face from the time you *had* a face. Your father would show us your pictures twice a year—the ones he'd take at Christmas, the ones from summer. Gail's got a picture of you framed on her dresser—the day you were commissioned. *(Looks to Paul)* Here he is and you were right.

GAIL

(To Logan) Now you'll get *stuck-up.*

PAUL

Let him. He deserves it.

LOGAN

(To Lena) I'm sorry.

Lena nods a dignified acceptance, a little surprised to find she has needed the apology for years.

GAIL

For what?

They all look to Gail but no one answers.

GAIL

(To Lena) I liked it—didn't you?

PAUL

(To Gail) She told him. Eat your pie.

GAIL

I'm sick of pie.

PAUL

(Smiles) The poor little Chinese children would love it.

GAIL

Then mail it to them. *(Pushes the plate in Paul's direction)*

LENA

I may let you take it to them—on foot through the water—if you don't cheer up.

GAIL

Gladly. Any place would be better.

Gail slumps in a sulk.

Paul is amused.

Lena is embarrassed.

Logan has finished his first slice of pie.

LOGAN

(Reaching out) I'm pitiful enough. Can I finish it for you?

Gail nods, still fuming, and Logan takes her plate.

LENA

You may get *rabies*, Logan.

LOGAN

I've had the shots—*one* thing the Army's good for.

Logan tries to eat comically—elaborate chewing.

Gail watches, unamused.

LOGAN

Found an old buddy of yours in the woods.

GAIL

(Reluctant) I don't have buddies.

PAUL

He found one anyhow.

GAIL

(To Logan) Who?

LOGAN

(Still eating) Long lost and miserable.

PAUL

Neglected and crippled.

LOGAN

Left for dead.

PAUL

Least she's out of her pain.

Gail is torn now between her prior sulk, her present curiosity and the fear of being tricked.

GAIL

I've never hurt anybody bad as that. *(Looks to Lena)*

LENA

(Raises hands in bafflement) Not so far as I know. Of course, you're grown now. There's a lot I don't see.

PAUL

This was the worst.

Gail is suddenly in tears—no sound, real pain.

All watch her a moment, surprised by their power to ruin her pleasure, but no one moves.

Gail faces Logan, still silent but asking relief from him.

Logan stands in place and beckons Gail to follow him out.

20

A quarter-hour later in the dark woods beside the creek.

Logan walks with a flashlight held before him.

Gail follows closely.

Logan turns into the ring, lays the light on the central stone (shining at the ground), kneels at the grave and digs with gentle hands. When he's found the doll again, he brushes at her face and holds her out to Gail.

Gail is reluctant but finally takes her by the leg, in one hand.

LOGAN

Remember now?

GAIL

Maybe so. There's a lot I forget.

LOGAN

Dad said you and he left it here when it broke.

He quickly smooths the dirt, then stands.

GAIL

He was always bringing me dolls—dolls, dolls. They were meant to make me like him.

LOGAN

Did they work?

GAIL

(Studies the doll's face) No. *(Touches the ruined eye)* I liked him anyway. We didn't get a whole lot of people through here—still don't, I told you. I like everybody I possibly can.

Logan smiles and steps back to sit on the center stone.

GAIL

Let's don't stay here please.

LOGAN

Got homework to do?

GAIL

(Nods) Latin—but that's not why.

LOGAN

(Smiles) Scared of Nazi bombers?

GAIL

(Laughs) I *used* to be. When the war first started, I thought every plane passing over at night had me in the bombsight. Now I doubt even *Germans* would want this place.

LOGAN

Seems nice to me.

GAIL

It's better right down by the creek.

LOGAN

I could build a fire here—

GAIL

(Suddenly firm) I said I couldn't stay here.

LOGAN

(Shrugs, gestures) Lead the way, Lady.

GAIL

Don't make fun. This is where I was miserable.

LOGAN

What happened here?

Gail pauses, then turns and walks from the ring. In three steps she's vanished.

Logan turns on the flashlight.

The doll lies skewed at his feet, dropped by Gail.

He stands, leaving it, and follows Gail.

She is kneeling on the creek bank, her right hand in the water.

Logan moves up beside her and stands four feet away.

LOGAN

Is it cold?

GAIL

No, warm for some reason. You can sit down here.

LOGAN

Thank you. I'm tired. *(Puts a hand in the water, pulls it back quickly)* Gail, it's cold as *glaciers*!

GAIL

I knew you wouldn't like it.

LOGAN

(Laughs) I just told a simple truth. *(Blows on his hand to warm it)*

GAIL

I used to love it here.

LOGAN

You said you were miserable.

GAIL

That's *why* I loved it. I came here and talked to what couldn't talk back—rocks, leaves, lizards, frogs.

LOGAN

What would you say?

GAIL

I'd ask for things—a life like everybody else: some sisters maybe.

LOGAN

Wouldn't God be the one to ask? Do lizards answer prayer?

GAIL

In stories, sure. No, we don't go to church; so God's not something I think much about.

LOGAN

Everybody else is—praying for peace. Stuff like that.

GAIL

God made lizards. They can carry the message.

LOGAN

They never do seem to have got you the *sisters.*

GAIL

Too late now.

LOGAN

Why?

GAIL

(Searches his face) Boy, where have you been?

LOGAN

All over—here to Idaho.

GAIL

I got you instead.

LOGAN

(Lost) Ma'm?

GAIL

You—not a sister.

LOGAN

(Smiles) Thank you, ma'm.

GAIL

Stuck-up—

LOGAN

O.K. then, I'm sorry.

GAIL

(Searches him again and leans a little closer) I'm not—any more.

She slowly leans farther.

Logans waits in place.

She brushes her lips against his, then retreats.

LOGAN

(Touching his mouth) You know I'm not your cousin?

GAIL

I know what they *told* me. *(Points toward the house)*

LOGAN

Do you think they've told us the whole truth now?

GAIL

I don't much care, do you?

Logan thinks, then reaches a hand toward her face. His thumb strokes her brow, smoothing the hairs again and again.

Gail accepts it calmly.

LOGAN

I guess I do—I plan to be a lawyer.

GAIL

People won't blame *you.*

LOGAN

(Smiles) I didn't mean that. I'll just need to know plain facts someday. I may have to manage all this if Dad dies.

GAIL

He won't. And forget about *facts*—I've been told more versions of them and who they are than the Bible tells of Moses and the Jews.

LOGAN

By Lena?

GAIL

(Nods) —They've known each other from the time they were *children*—they never saw each other till after I was born—you used to live with us when I was a *baby*—we're cousins; we're not—we're sister and br—

Logan stops her with a hand to her lips

They stay a moment silent. Then they sit back a little from one another.

Logan lies back on the ground.

LOGAN

(To the dark trees above) Let's let the facts wait.

GAIL

For what?

LOGAN

To see if I get back.

GAIL

From where?

LOGAN

Wherever I go tomorrow—home to my mother's old house, then Idaho, then the whole blue Pacific, then God knows where.

GAIL

What if you don't?

LOGAN

Lena said I would.

GAIL

Lena says a lot—she's a *schoolteacher*, Logan. They can talk lawyers down.

Logan takes that in silence, staring up.

Gail moves over, knees almost against his side.

He reaches blindly for her wrist, lays her hand on the center of his chest.

They stay thus, silent. Then—

LOGAN

You've talked *me* down anyhow. You a teacher too?

GAIL

No, I'm a doctor. *(Feels for his heart, then counts the beats)* One—two—three—four. *You're* still alive.

LOGAN

And strong?

GAIL

—As a bear.

LOGAN

But with much better manners.

GAIL

I thought people didn't have to have manners now—the war and all.

LOGAN

Well, *war*time manners. I try to have those.

Gail nods but stays in place, her hand now flat on his heart.

Logan reaches slowly for the crown of her head and bends that gently toward him.

Gail stops the move eight inches from his lips and searches his eyes.

GAIL

You sure about this?

LOGAN

No.

GAIL

What if you come back?

LOGAN

Then I'll have to *get* sure. I'll be another man.

Gail waits a long moment.

Then his hand brings her lightly to rest on his lips—a long still kiss.

21

A half-hour later in Lena's dark yard, the bottom of the kitchen steps.

Gail and Logan approach, close but not touching.

The porch light is on—and a dim glow from the kitchen—but the house is silent.

Gail takes the lead to climb the steps.

Logan hooks a finger in the back of her belt, stops and turns her. He studies her face.

LOGAN

I'll say goodbye here.

GAIL

I'll see you at breakfast.

LOGAN

I guess we'll push on. Dad has to work tomorrow.

GAIL

The nearest hotel is thirty miles east, and it'll be shut down tight by now. This isn't *Idaho.*

LOGAN

You got room here?

GAIL

I'll sleep with Mother. You and Paul can have my room.

LOGAN

He may not want that.

GAIL

(Nods) He will.

LOGAN

I won't sleep a minute—he snores like a walrus.

GAIL

Sleep's a big superstition. Some weeks I don't sleep an hour all-told.

LOGAN

Will you tonight?

GAIL

(Thinks) I might have to dream. *(Looks toward the woods)* Have you got an address?

LOGAN

It may change soon.

GAIL

I guess Paul'll know it.

LOGAN

So will you.

GAIL

O.K.

She smiles mildly and turns to go in.

LOGAN

Goodbye though.

GAIL

(Smiling) O.K.

She reaches down and touches his forehead lightly.

Then she turns and climbs quickly toward the kitchen.

22

Immediately after in Lena's kitchen.

The room is clean of all traces of supper. The only light is from a kerosene lamp on the central table.

In its glow Lena sits at the table, marking student papers.

As Gail and Logan enter, Lena looks up—tired but suppressing anxiety.

LENA

(To Gail) Which one was it?—Ethel?

Gail stops, three steps into the room, baffled by the question.

LENA

—The poor dead doll. Was it Ethel or Maxine?

GAIL

It must have been Patricia, but she's pretty far gone.

LENA

I trust you reinterred her.

LOGAN

She's all right. She won't feel a thing.

LENA

Miss Gail Brock won't be feeling much either if she doesn't tuck into that Latin homework.

GAIL

Can I work in your room?

LENA

Help yourself—just *work.*

Gail nods and moves to leave the room.

LENA

Tell Logan "Good night."

GAIL

I already did.

Not looking again to Logan, she leaves.

He smiles to her back as she vanishes in the hall. Then he slowly looks to Lena.

LOGAN

Where's Dad?

LENA

In the living room, snoozing on the world's worst sofa.

LOGAN

Is there some kind of plan about where we spend the night?

LENA

(Laughs a little) Nothing under *this* roof was ever planned. But you're welcome here.

LOGAN

Thank you. If he's already out, we'd better just leave him.

LENA

You sleepy?

LOGAN

No ma'm. I'm on Idaho time.

LENA

Would a cup of coffee kill you?

LOGAN

I doubt it.

LENA

Sit down then.

She sweeps the papers to one side, stands, goes to the stove and pours two cups of coffee.

Logan takes the chair opposite hers.

She returns, puts the coffee down and sits again.

LOGAN

(Points to the oil lamp) You blow a fuse in here?

LENA

No, I just like to work by oil light. Takes me back to my log-cabin youth. May become the first woman president this way. *(Sips her coffee)*

LOGAN

You're from South Carolina?

LENA

(Nods) I was—back before man invented the wheel. Paul tell you my history?

LOGAN

A little—before supper.

LENA

It didn't spoil your appetite.

LOGAN

No'm. I'm trained to eat under fire.

LENA

Was it that bad?

LOGAN

(Thinks) At first. *(Nods)*

LENA

I'm sorry. It was Paul's idea, not mine.

LOGAN

See, I miss my mother—I told you that. I tried not to say a real goodbye to her when I left for Idaho—she was such a deep worrier—so now all I've got is: *she's* the one that's pulled out and left me standing on the platform waving and hoping she'll look back one last time.

LENA

She would, if they'd give her the chance. But my aunt used to say "When they take you fast, they're proving they love you."

LOGAN

(Thinks) They must be nuts about young boys then.

LENA

I said you'd be safe. I know it in my bones.

LOGAN

(Studies her, smiles slightly, nods) Then I won't doubt your word.

LENA

—Lena. Call me Lena please.

LOGAN

All right. *(Waits, swallows coffee)* Lena—what did my mother know about you?

Lena has dreaded that but takes it almost calmly.

She reaches for a student paper. On its clean back she begins writing lines of Palmer Method exercises—circles and spikes.

LENA

Paul used to say *nothing*. She'd never asked a question or showed a sign of worry. That was way back at the start. I haven't asked—oh—since Gail learned to talk.

LOGAN

He was right—it never changed. She'd have told me if she'd known.

LENA

(Scrawls a moment more, then looks up) I won't doubt your word. *(Smiles)* But it's hard *not* to. All my life I've had this curse— *(Quickly she cups hands over her eyes, then uncovers them again)* I can see through time. Maybe it comes from working with children all my adult life; but I know what people think, whatever they tell me.

LOGAN

And you've told *me* the truth?

LENA

(Nods) You'll never leave Idaho, except to come home.

LOGAN

Then what's he thinking? *(Points toward the living room)*

LENA

Paul? He's numb right now—I don't mean his nap. He loved your mother too. He'll be lost for a while. Then he'll ask my opinion.

LOGAN

On what?

LENA

Where his home is, how he'll live from here on.

LOGAN

He'll move here with you.

LENA

(Thinks, shakes her head) Too many questions here. There's plenty little towns to get lost in. They all have schools; all need pianos. *(Smiles)*

LOGAN

Do you want that?—moving again, seeing more of Paul, a family Christmas?

LENA

(Thinks) Funny *you* should ask. Paul never has. For all I know, he may not.

LOGAN

He will. He told me. He wanted my blessing.

LENA

That was too much to ask for—*this* week, at least.

LOGAN

He's always assumed I was strong as he. He means it as a compliment.

LENA

You will be.

LOGAN

I am.

LENA

(Nods unsmiling) Did you bless him then?

Logan takes a swallow of coffee. Then—almost somnambulistic—he rises, goes to the sink, empties the cup, runs water till it's cold. Then he bends and drinks directly from the stream. He stands, dries his lips with the back of his hand and stares out the window toward the dimly lit yard.

LOGAN

Not yet, I don't guess.

LENA

Is my coffee that bad? *(Smiles)*

LOGAN

(His back still to Lena) No, I was thirsty. *(Turns and faces her, studies her face)* How have you borne this?

LENA

I won't say it's been my favorite *day.*

LOGAN

I meant the whole last—what?—seventeen years.

LENA

I'm tough and not too bright.

LOGAN

Both lies. I can *see. (Touches his eyes)*

LENA

Well, I told them to myself—nobody else till you.

LOGAN

You've been claiming to tell me trustworthy facts.

LENA

(Thinks, nods) Excuse me. O.K. This is bedrock *fact*—it's been so bad at times I'd have killed myself if there hadn't been Gail.

LOGAN

He'd have seen to Gail.

LENA

He wouldn't. He told me. See, I tried it once. The Christmas she was two years old and asked for him—the next time he stopped here, I *went* for myself.

She holds up her left wrist—a long white scar.

Logan studies it from a distance.

Then he slowly comes to the table, sits and extends a finger to touch the scar.

Lena takes it back and wipes it on her lips.

LENA

As soon as the blood stopped, he sat me down right here at this table and said, very calmly, "You were grown when you met me. You knew my life but you took me on. Gail followed from that. If you plan to leave her, find a home for her first—she can't come with me."

LOGAN

He said it that plain?

LENA

Verbatim, more or less.

LOGAN

And you stayed on.

LENA

I guess I did. *(Again she rubs the scarred wrist, with her right hand)* I seem to be the same person anyhow, most days.

LOGAN

(Shakes his head) God—

LENA

I haven't finished yet. *(Smiles)* You asked for the truth. Why I'm *here* at all—why Gail is in my room conjugating Latin—is because Paul Melton is asleep on the couch in that dark living room. *(Points)* He's a gentle person, with the time he's had. And he's all I've wanted. Something put me in his path nearly half my life ago. We've enjoyed each other, whoever we hurt. And *we'll* pay for that, nobody else now.

LOGAN

What about Gail and me?

LENA

Gail'll be gone soon—two or three more years—some boy of her own. I can't stop that. *(Waits, searches Logan's eyes)* You've gone already—on your own life, I mean. You're strong as us or stronger. If we ever hurt you, it's over now.

LOGAN

(Nods) I hope you're right. *(Waits, then smiles)* You throwing us out?

LENA

(Quickly) Lord, no. You're welcome wherever we are—if we end up together.

LOGAN

You will. Paul Melton can't stay alone long.

LENA

I don't know that. Anything else he's wanted, he's managed to have. Being lonely is just a simple skill. You can learn it if you want to.

LOGAN

I don't think I do.

LENA

(Serious) I didn't mean you. I just preach to *myself.*

LOGAN

(Smiles) In what church? I'd like to join your church.

LENA

(Begins to calm) I call it The Church of Getting Through Time. No, Gail goes along to the Methodists sometime. I don't have the gall.

They do not know it yet, but they have answered their questions about one another. The stream between them runs relatively clear.

Logan pushes back from the table with his hands, rocks on the hind legs of his chair and stares up at the ceiling—the dim warm flicker of shadow from the lamp.

Lena reaches for the papers again and begins to sort them.

Logan looks down at last.

LOGAN

I'll leave you to work.

LENA

(Smiles) Where would you go?—we've got a full house.

LOGAN

I'll wake Dad up. *(Looks to his watch)* We can listen to the news.

LENA

I could fix you a snack.

LOGAN

(Standing) You grade your papers. Maybe after that.

Lena nods and reaches to take her red pencil.

Logan moves toward the hall door. He stops on the threshold and turns back to Lena.

Her eyes are still on him.

LENA

I haven't lied to you.

LOGAN

I believe you. I'll be back.

He turns again and takes three steps into the dark hall. Then he stops and returns.

Lena still faces him.

LOGAN

You know I loved my mother?

LENA

It's one of the main things I'll know from now on.

Logan waits a moment, nods, gives a little parting wave and leaves again.

Lena watches him out of sight, then turns up her lamp and takes a student paper.

23

Immediately after in Lena's living room.

Logan comes to the open door and stops, the dim hall behind him.

The living room is only lit by the filtered shine from a street lamp.

Paul is on the sofa—on his back, his head propped awkwardly on an old felt pillow. His face is obscured, and Logan cannot be sure he's asleep.

LOGAN

(Half-volume, from the doorway) Dad?

No answer. Paul doesn't move.

LOGAN

(Slightly louder) Sir—

Paul's hand flicks once at his face—a fly—but still no answer. Then a thin strain of snoring grinds out.

Logan smiles, takes a step in and looks round the room—a small upright piano in a corner. Logan silently moves toward it and sits on the bench. He looks once more to Paul—still snoring.

Then he turns to the keys, poises a moment and begins the Chopin Prelude in D Flat (the one Gail had played). He plays it note-perfect, deeply felt.

The entire piece consumes a little more than four minutes. In its course, and responding to its varying moods, the following silent actions occur.

Paul gradually wakes, looks over to Logan, studies his profile, then sits up and rubs his own eyes. He rises and goes to stand behind Logan. He is close but does not touch him.

In the darkest passage of the music, Gail appears in the doorway. She stops there—disheveled from studying—and watches the two men's backs. Her face is nearly blank.

Neither Paul nor Logan turn to see her.

A few seconds from the end of the piece, Lena appears. She stops behind Gail, again not touching, and listens calmly.

At the last note, Logan's hands stay on the keys. He has sensed his father's nearness but has not heard the women.

PAUL

(In place, not moving) She'd have been very proud.

LOGAN

(To the keys) I practice when I can.

Paul opens his right hand and lays it broadly on the crown of Logan's head.

Logan does not turn but shuts his eyes and smiles very slightly.

Gail gently applauds.

Lena moves to restrain her.

Paul looks back; Logan does not.

PAUL

Is it *day* already?

Gail turns to Lena.

Lena takes a step forward.

Logan turns on the bench and looks back.

LENA

(Shakes her head) Barely bedtime. That was beautiful, Logan.

Logan nods acceptance.

LENA

I promised you a snack.

PAUL

Any walnut pie left?

LENA

Not a crumb.

PAUL

Any eggs?

LENA

Two dozen—

PAUL

I'll make a cheese omelet.

GAIL

Then *nobody* would sleep.

Paul smiles and begins to move toward the door.

PAUL

Nothing wrong with that—sleep's a big superstition; you been saying so for years.

He passes the women and vanishes toward the kitchen.

Lena watches his back in mild exasperation, then follows him.

Gail and Logan face each other.

He stays on the bench.

Gail advances to the center of the room.

Logan takes another long look at her face.

Then he slowly turns to the keys again and plays the Bach Prelude in C.

FULL MOON

F O R

XANDER BERKELEY

For stages with elaborate machinery, I suggest a few details of design. But scenic considerations never slow a fluid progress through the nearly continuous action. A unit set, with a minimum of authentic decor, is likely to be sufficient—the Bascomb house to one side, the Patrick house to the other, the Gaskin house perhaps between and behind the two. A loosely defined but consistent use of three separate areas, with a minimum of furniture, is equally possible. Avoid Southern stereotypes—white-columned grandeur or hillbilly shacks. A large white, or whitewashed, rock stands near the center.

The speech of all characters is a heightened version of the language of a particular civilization at a particular time. It is a tongue in which people say, or conceal, their urgent meanings with unusual directness and power. No group of citizens ever spoke with such consistent ease and adequacy; but then the Aran Islanders on whom Synge based his plays hardly spoke at the sustained poetic pitch he reared on the base of their inherent eloquence, not to speak of the volubility and grace of all the Hamlets and both the Macbeths.

If actors are not familiar with subtleties of upper-class white and middle-class black accents in eastern North Carolina in the 1930s, they should not risk a reckless substitution of other "Southern" dialects—especially not the mountain or Ozark hillbilly accent which is generally, and disastrously, offered by non-Southerners. Far better to employ a generic non-urban American pronunciation and rhythm. Pay attention to the built-in rhythms of the dialogue and the cumulative build of longer speeches. Elide the *-ing* endings on participles and adjectives, and remember always that the dialects of the American South are founded upon the first principle of courteous discourse everywhere—be as clear and entertaining as truth and brevity allow. Boredom is a prime sin, and a pleasingly rhythmic delivery is the aim of all. Black house-servants and most upper-class whites pride themselves on fluency in one another's dialects and gestures.

It is likewise a society in which shouting matches almost never occur. Men and women, white and black, respond to life with a quick high intensity. But in their personal encounters—and especially in inter-racial contacts—a harshly raised voice is seldom heard. The passion is conveyed by rhythm, emphasis and body-English, not by loudness. As in Chekhov or Japanese Noh plays, that courtly suppression and control of anger adds all the more power to human transactions. A family of brawling New Jersey dockhands would envy the force of this slow emotional pressure.

The black characters must never lapse into demeaning stereotypes. Though still a servant class at the time of the action, these are self-esteeming and dignified citizens. Sarah Gaskin and Walter Parker are firmly aware of their indispensability in the homes where they work. Ora Lee Gaskin, being younger, begins to show a newer impatience. In each case, despite a three-century-old intimacy with their overlords, the people stubbornly continue to feed their dimming African memories into the prevailing Anglo-Saxon and Celtic language and customs.

Clothing for all the white characters is of good, though not luxurious or voguish, quality. Again avoid Southern stereotypes—no white linen suits and string ties for the men, no picture-hats for the women. The three black characters, working in or related to white homes, are spared the wardrobe depredations of the Great Depression, which is only beginning to relent.

The time—late summer—implies intense heat and humidity, with a consequent slowness in movement and speech.

Popular band and vocal music of the time—jazz and swing, mixed with black gospel and blues of the same near-desperate period—may be used to strong effect, provided it never drowns a speech.

R.P.

CHARACTERS

KERNEY BASCOMB - *age 19, unmarried and unemployed*

KIPPLE PATRICK - *age 21, a clerk in the local Savings and Loan*

JOHN BASCOMB - *late 40s, Kerney's father, a widower and a lawyer*

WALTER PARKER - *mid-30s, black, cook and general butler to the Bascombs*

SARAH GASKIN - *mid-40s, black, cook and maid to the Patricks, and Ora Lee's mother*

ORA LEE GASKIN - *age 22, black, Sarah's daughter and a former intimate of Kip's*

FRANK PATRICK - *late 40s, Kip's father, a widower and a high-school Latin teacher*

CHRISTINE BASCOMB - *Kerney's mother and John's wife, seen as a young woman in Kerney's dream*

DOROTHY PATRICK - *Kip's mother and Frank's wife, also seen as a young woman in Kerney's dream*

PLACE

Eastern North Carolina

TIME

Late summer 1938

SCENES

Act One

1. *The Bascomb yard*
2. *The Bascomb kitchen*
3. *The Gaskin yard*
4. *The Bascomb yard*
5. *The Patrick porch*
6. *Kerney's dream*

Act Two

1. *The Bascomb kitchen*
2. *The Patrick porch*
3. *The Gaskin yard*
4. *The Patrick porch*

ACT ONE

1

Saturday, near midnight. The empty yard of a handsome but respectably disheveled house with doorsteps and porch. One huge tree shades the yard from the light of a powerful full moon, but one shaft penetrates the leaves and throws a focused brightness on the ground.

Offstage, the sound of a car door closing; then a second door.

Kerney Bascomb and Kipple Patrick enter in party clothes—a calf-length clinging dress for Kerney, a seersucker suit and loosened tie for Kip.

Kip goes to the central white rock and sits exhausted.

But Kerney is restless and moves into the moonlight. In the phosphorescent center she stops and looks up, bathing her face.

Throughout they speak with a hushed intensity. Respectful of the hour and her father's nearness, they rarely raise their voices.

KERNEY

(Hugging her shoulders and shivering) This moonlight has got to be *poison.* Everybody knows it'll drive you crazy. *(Waits, bathes her face again in the glow)* I may already be stark raving nuts. And it's not just the gin—

KIP

Kerney, you were crazy before they *had* moonlight.

KERNEY

Crazy enough to stay in this town—a Christian white lady with nothing to do, locked up indoors. *(Sees the moon again)* How can people sleep through something fine as this?

KIP

They get as tired as I am now. And you're no lady.

KERNEY

(Stepping toward him) I begin to believe you. And oh sweet Kip, you're too old for me. I'm awake; every cell of my body is singing. And thus I bid you a grateful good night. *(Gives an elaborate bow, nearly falls, then continues toward him)*

KIP

Stay. Stay *there.*

KERNEY

If you don't want me, there's others that do—lady or tramp.

KIP

Lady, I want you but I want you *there*, this instant. *(Studies her)* Kerney Bascomb, you - look - so - fine.

Kerney is puzzled for a moment, then moves through a light succession of poses, a silent fluid dance.

Then she stops and stands, facing Kip.

KIP

I - *need* - it.

KERNEY

It? Be ashamed. Anyhow, you're familiar with my *it.*

KIP

Forgive me, lady. I want you forever.

KERNEY

I'm no fine lady trapped in your dream. Since school, I've spent a whole two years as a trainee lady—indoor sports like reading novels and having headaches, going out just to weddings and dances.

KIP

(Waits, then stands) You look too good. I may need to join you.

KERNEY

You - are - not - hearing - me. You told me to *stay.* Didn't we promise not to touch anymore, not till we know?

KIP

I know. I need you.

KERNEY

We both said we wanted to think awhile.

KIP

Maybe my advanced age speeded me up. And this fine moonlight and you resigning your ladyhood.

KERNEY

A former lady's not always a tramp.

KIP

You know what I mean.

KERNEY

I honest to God don't know if I do. You're an older man. Hell, I'm just nineteen.

Kip moves toward Kerney. Through the rest of the meeting, they move round the yard—standing or sitting on the white rock—till they end on the porch steps.

Before he speaks again, Kip extends a slow hand toward her.

Kerney gives no sign of shying, but his reach barely misses contact, and he chooses not to step closer.

KIP

I've looked far ahead as my eyes reach. And Kerney, I want us to leave here soon and marry each other.

KERNEY

We could always leave and marry other people.

KIP

(With sudden calm force) Don't talk that trash.

KERNEY

(Calm too) I'll say any goddamned thing I feel.

KIP

Your father'll hear us.

KERNEY

My pa could teach us worlds about swearing.

KIP

All your pa wants to teach Kip is *running* lessons—how to run as far as Bangor, Maine and never see you.

KERNEY

And your pa's not that stuck on me.

KIP

That's a lie. He told me, not two days ago, "Kip, she's an elegant piece of construction with a mind like a steel trap. Don't let her vanish."

KERNEY

(Laughs and nods) Your pa would call a two-headed cross-eyed brunette gorgeous if she kept you home.

KIP

We wouldn't live with him.

KERNEY

But in sight and earshot.

KIP

McDuff is no village. We'd move across town—

KERNEY

Across the tracks maybe? *(Half-sings)* Out near Sugartown, where the sweet darkies dwell—

KIP

(Ignoring her hint and fervent to hide the problem she has raised) Kerney, my father's been good to me. Now he faces me leaving. I don't see you abandoning yours.

Kerney thinks through that. It is the first time she has faced the full prospect of leaving home. Her face slowly mirrors the mind's desolation. At no other moment will she seem more alone.

When she speaks, she's resolved.

KERNEY

I - *will* - leave - though, when the time really comes.

At the end she is smiling.

Kip sees it, shivers slightly.

KIP

Got any hint who you're leaving with?

KERNEY

I've entertained more than one bid and you know it. Yours still in force?

KIP

(Waits incredulous) God on high, woman! Kipple Patrick loves you. He's said it all ways, in more than one language, since you were a child.

KERNEY

Ego amo te. Je t'aime. Yo te amo. And what about African? Mumby-Jumby-Boo! I'll need to learn it in African, won't I?—to keep your attention.

KIP

You're not drunk. Why the hell turn vicious?

Kerney takes fire from his word vicious. *She waits blankly for a moment, then contorts her face and gives a sudden, muted but impressive cat's warning growl and a single clawing gesture in the air.*

KERNEY

(Suddenly calm) Something mean got in me, some truth-telling demon.

KIP

Get it out fast.

Kerney prowls in the effort to clear her mind. She has a fierce need to exorcise what she has heard in town gossip but has not discussed with Kip.

KERNEY

I need to hear you say it again. Make your bid again please.

KIP

You're not at auction. It's a heartfelt proposal.

KERNEY

Say it.

KIP

(Waits) Let's clear out of here. We'll catch a train to South Carolina, get married down there where you don't need a blood test and spare our fathers the cost and worry. What we save, we can put toward buying a house.

KERNEY

Sounds easy as buying a red toothbrush.

KIP

It's not that new an invention, girl—holy matrimony. A man and a woman choose each other and say so in public. Ninety people in any odd hundred have done it.

KERNEY

A hundred people in any odd hundred are going to die. I don't think I plan to be that normal.

KIP

You won't be normal—don't lose sleep on it.

KERNEY

Now tell me why I should do what you say?

KIP

Say *we* for once. Why should *we* elope?

KERNEY

I'm all *for* elopement. Big weddings are nothing but a sinful waste. No, tell me why to get married at all. And why is it holy?

Through the following Kerney reveals a genuine innocence—she does not know and wants to.

Kip shows the delighted patience of a good teacher.

KIP

I guess most girls learn this from their mothers, so you got left out. But I just thought—Lord, with all we've done, from rafters to floor—you were some great expert on love and life.

KERNEY

I did what you and Jeffer Burns taught me. It didn't seem holy.

KIP

Don't mention Jeffer Burns. *(Waits)* You enjoyed yourself, true?

KERNEY

I liked being present and helping you out. It seemed like something you needed, right then, to go on living. Like you were out to get my blood.

KIP

I never meant harm.

KERNEY

Never—you didn't. It *seemed* like, seemed that urgent.

KIP

And it's not for you? I'm a young man, girl. Men are built that way. But hurt you? God, I want you to last—here in my life.

KERNEY

Why not another girl—same hills and valleys—that can cook, clean house, do long division? I can't walk straight, much less keep house.

KIP

You, Kerney. You or life alone.

KERNEY

I'm looking at life alone myself. *(Waits, laughs)* If I die tonight you'd marry by fall.

KIP

Me and my wife'll sweep the dead leaves off you.

KERNEY

(Laughs) See?

KIP

—If you're *dead.* But if you're drawing breath on Earth—with Jeffer Burns or Gary-damned-Cooper—I'll be the most miserable soul upright.

KERNEY

Is it holy though? Why won't you tell me?

KIP

(Waits, then smiles) I can't say I'd ask God to watch every minute. But I think he blesses love, lasting love.

KERNEY

Church love, altar love. Church marriage makes you say "Forsaking all others." You ready for that?

KIP

I've copied the Methodist marriage vows. Once we're joined by the justice of peace, we'll read each other the vows in private.

KERNEY

You didn't! *(Laughs)* If I know you, there'll be precious little reading. But "Forsaking all others"—talk about that.

KIP

Who's been filling your head with filth? I'll come to you clean.

KERNEY

(With increasing force) I've heard that concubines flourish hereabouts. I'll need an oath that I'm all you've got before I let my

body start babies. *(Tries to lighten her tone)* Now if we perform this private wedding in our honeymoon nest, will you sing "Oh, Promise Me" and other crowd favorites? *(Then quickly)* Kipple, Kipple—I don't mean to mock. God knows, you can't marry me in church. Orange blossoms and satin just will not hang on skin as wicked as this skin has been.

Kip thinks, then gently takes Kerney's wrist, kisses it, trails his lips delicately up the skin.

KIP

Sweet, sweet, sweet.

Kerney bears him a moment, then pulls away—no harshness or fear.

She walks to the dark edge of the pool of moonlight.

Kip moves to follow.

She stops him with a gesture, then studies him.

KERNEY

Kip Patrick, I may need you.

KIP

Is that the same as "Kip, I may love you"?

KERNEY

It could well be—any minute, any day.

KIP

You're welcome to phone me collect, from any phone on the planet Earth, if and when you can truly say yes.

KERNEY

I can save you some cash— *(Faces him fully)*

Kip is oddly cautious. He waits a moment, then steps to within an arm's length of her.

She pulls him down to sit beside her.

KERNEY

I want to try what you think is right. *(Reaches for his hand)*

KIP

Kerney, I'm overwhelmed but—hell!—we're in plain view of your father's window.

Kerney takes Kip's wrist and repeats his kisses.

Kip accepts with less than total joy—quick glances at the house.

Ending her kisses at his elbow, Kerney smiles in his face and slowly stands.

KERNEY

We both need sleep.

KIP

Hold on, sweet child—you got me tuned up tight as a harp string. If I break now and lash around, I'll leave thousands homeless.

KERNEY

That's what I said—we both need rest.

KIP

(Waits) Can I take you to church in the morning?

KERNEY

Won't the church cave in?

She backs away almost into darkness, then blows a slow kiss.

KIP

Did you mean all this?

KERNEY

Every word, all night—in spite of this moon.

KIP

Then let's leave now. In less than a day, we can be man and—

KERNEY

(Smiles) Slow down, boy. I can't have you locked in jail—hauling a minor across state lines.

KIP

Nineteen is grown.

Kerney by now is almost dark.

KERNEY

No sir, not yet—twenty-two long months. Go take a cold swim for two more years. You need exercise.

KIP

(Whispers) You need not to never drink gin again.

KERNEY

This is on *your* soul. *(Then a Mae West imitation)* I'm a child, big boy. *(A distinct pause, then trailing off in her own voice)* A jealous child that demands every drop of your heart's blood and will not share it with any live thing—

The dim sight and sound of Kerney withdrawing, climbing the porch steps, opening the door.

Kip clenches his hands in confusion and leaves.

2

Twelve-fifteen a.m. The kitchen of the Bascomb house.

Lights rise as Kerney enters the door. She surveys the room, then busies herself to pick up a fallen newspaper, straighten a picture and turn off the radio.

From a big armchair in a corner, with its back to the audience, a concealed man suddenly stands into view. He is Kerney's father, John Bascomb.

JOHN

Evening.

KERNEY

(Surprised) Thought you were long since dead to the world.

JOHN

(Smiles) That's in the hands of fate, sweetheart. I was waiting for you.

KERNEY

I'm here—no major parts missing, I guess. *(Looks down)*

JOHN

(Turns his chair and sits again) How was the dance?

KERNEY

(Matter of factly) Awful, as expected. Half the boys passed out. The other half stripped and jumped in the pond. More than one girl joined them.

JOHN

Not naked?

KERNEY

Not in hoopskirts.

JOHN

And not including you, I trust—or Jeffer Burns?

KERNEY

Pa, Jefferson Burns left three weeks ago.

JOHN

Bless his bones, wherever he is.

KERNEY

He can't be dead. His mother says he writes.

JOHN

Were you that mean to him?

KERNEY

(Waits) Jeffer said he would kill himself if I turned down the diamond he bought. I knew his mother had paid the deposit, but it was a stunner—canary yellow.

JOHN

They're the costliest kind.

KERNEY

But if I put yellow next to my skin, I closely resemble a killed dressed chicken.

JOHN

So you declined?

KERNEY

I wore it ten minutes, to say I had. Then I politely handed it back. Jeffer said "I'm going to kill myself this Saturday night." That was a Wednesday. He had a big week ahead at the store and would have to wait for the weekend to die. So I felt safe refusing.

JOHN

(Waits) You were wrong.

KERNEY

I was wrong.

They both pause silently, recalling Jeffer.

Then both break up.

KERNEY

Stole his mother's best car and two fur coats and drove to *Arkansas*!

JOHN

Didn't know they had roads between here and there.

KERNEY

They don't! That was half of Jeff's point—he wanted that bad to never see me.

JOHN

He'll forget and drift back.

KERNEY

He'd have to eat about two tons of crow.

JOHN

(Waits, smiles) You break all hearts.

KERNEY

(Laughs) What has got into boys? I'm nothing but an ordinary girl with straight teeth—a slight overbite—nice table manners, can't toast a marshmallow much less cook a meal and about as interested in true romance as a black widow spider.

JOHN

(Studies her slowly) You're a certified beauty.

KERNEY

Who signed the certificate?

JOHN

Your father—his name is first anyhow.

KERNEY

(Laughs) Shoot!

But she rises quickly, goes to a mirror and reads her own face.

KERNEY

I can see Mother's good eyes. And lucky teeth. But look at this mole. *(Draws a line down the middle of her face)* And the halves don't match. I'm bigger on the left—

JOHN

You've said girls spend too much time on their looks.

KERNEY

I'm trying to see what has driven two otherwise sane men looney.

JOHN

Two—who else?

KERNEY

Kip Patrick, tonight.

JOHN

Did Kipple offend you?

KERNEY

Calm your heart, no sir. But time we get to the end of a date, Kip's way past ready to bake and serve.

JOHN

Better not tell your pa all that's true. Your mother taught you morals. She died before you needed them, but I'm sure you recall.

KERNEY

(Mock alarm) You speaking of passion?

JOHN

(Nods, smiling) And all its punishments.

KERNEY

Two-headed babies and tertiary syphillis.

JOHN

(Gentle but firm) Curb that mouth before it kills you. You know what I mean.

Kerney goes to a straight chair, some distance from her father.

At first she beams her broadest grin, but quickly it fails.

In another few seconds she is almost in tears.

KERNEY

I'm really not pregnant and I know you're a man but help - me - please. *(Real tears)*

John rises in place, takes a step toward her.

Kerney waves him back.

He comes anyhow, lays a white handkerchief in her lap, touches the crown of her head for five seconds, then returns to his chair.

She dries her eyes and strains for composure.

KERNEY

I'm a little bit drunk.

JOHN

What else is wrong?

KERNEY

I'm not expecting, Pa—that's the truth, not a baby at least. *(Waits)* I'm waiting—*waiting*—for life to start.

JOHN

I was under the impression, for nineteen years, that you were breathing nicely.

KERNEY

(Shakes her head) These last two years have been one *held* breath. See, I didn't understand that school was a *job*. It kept me busy as a bee in clover. And I got steady praise, which was better than pay. But now I feel like a Russian princess under house arrest with pernicious anemia. Not going *nowhere*, not learning a thing a chimpanzee couldn't learn in a day.

JOHN

I offered you college—St. Mary's, Sweetbriar.

KERNEY

(Nods) And I'm grateful. But who wants to hole up with a big bunch of girls just *parked* for four years, waiting till some boy jumps their engine and drives to the altar?

JOHN

You're grown in my eyes—your mind's a lot clearer, your face gets better by the hour. I've praised you daily—

KERNEY

This is not about you. It's me, me, me. And all I'm doing is lounging around on the doorstep of marriage till some boy, that doesn't quite turn my stomach, pops the question and I say "Why not?"

JOHN

I guess it *is* rough on a young woman's pride.

KERNEY

Pride *nothing*—it's rough on my behind. Sitting here, by the year, just sitting.

JOHN

Learn how to walk—take long brisk walks. Or learn a skill—like needlepoint. Visit the sick. Improve your mind.

KERNEY

I've improved my mind to the point it could almost invent electricity if Ben Franklin hadn't.

JOHN

(Calm but new to the subject) Have I failed that badly?

Kerney waits a long moment.

Her eyes fill again. She smiles and slowly nods her head Yes.

KERNEY

See, once Mother died, nobody made me want to be a woman. Nobody showed me that being a wife and mother was something a girl ought to *learn.*

JOHN

(Waits, then begins his defense) The morning she died, your mother sat up in the chair in our room—you'd gone to school. She meant me to hear her last requests—the clothes to be buried in, her recipe for mints (she promised it to Bailey years before but had always forgot). I wrote it all down, afraid to meet her eyes. But finally she said "John, look at me. The thing I cannot even *say* is, how scared I am to leave a girl child alone in this world." I told her I'd get the finest help and that I wasn't all that bad a father.

KERNEY

You haven't been.

JOHN

(Stops her with a gesture) She drew a great picture in the air with her hand—she was trying to make me see her fear. It ruined what was left of her face—that she was leaving you. And she wouldn't say your name; we'd both break down. So I said

"Christine, your daughter and mine will *count* in the world." I don't think it helped her.

KERNEY

You never told me that much before.

JOHN

I never saw I'd failed so badly.

Kerney reaches a hand in his direction.

John shakes his head No.

JOHN

I went on about my grown man's life and left you here to grow like ivy.

KERNEY

(Smiles) Did I grow that badly?

JOHN

I think you look fine. You're saying otherwise.

KERNEY

I'm saying that—whether I'm here at home or dancing fast in a crowd of boys—I see how lonesome I've been as a *girl*. And now I don't know why I should sit here and wait for a boy to stop by and take me.

JOHN

You can live in this house till it blows to dust.

KERNEY

(Shakes her head firmly) I need to leave. But where the hell to?

JOHN

Omit the extraneous syllables, darling. Makes your mouth look coarse.

KERNEY

I'm earnest, Pa.

JOHN

(Waits) Kip Patrick proposed.

KERNEY

Sir?

JOHN

Tonight, I'm guessing—Kip asked for your hand.

KERNEY

He's asked for several more parts, believe me. *(Extends her left hand and studies it)* Can you see me married?

JOHN

In general or to Kip?

KERNEY

Try it with Kip.

JOHN

(Waits) He's never been *arrested.*

KERNEY

Treat me better than that.

JOHN

I buried my mother thirty-two years ago. We buried yours eight years ago. So Kerney, don't ask me to cooperate in losing the last live woman I've got. *(Smiles finally)*

KERNEY

Pa, you can remarry any *day*. Mother told you that toward the end. I heard her.

JOHN

She did. And it pained me badly. Even young as you were, I knew I had you. And I wouldn't share that.

KERNEY

Thank you, sir. *(Waits)* I wish you hadn't said it.

JOHN

You've known it though. Any single father that's missed his chance to watch a daughter grow has missed life's most complicated rose hedge—one glorious bloom defended by one zillion poisonous thorns.

KERNEY

Whoa, John Bascomb! What are the thorns?

JOHN

You're a scholar, darling. Think about it. Trouble with me is, I longed to write poetry—how to say all you mean so nobody hears you. It still beats in me when I see the right face.

KERNEY

Those rhymes at bedtime—they were all yours?

John nods slowly.

KERNEY

(Remembering)

"A lonely man searched the wild,
Found a lady, they made a child.
Royal child, sink now to sleep.
We will guard you through the deep."

JOHN

I said I longed to write. I never said I triumphed. It's one thing to stand up talking in court. Or to face a working machine gun in France, but writing poems takes a daring mind. Got to stand up there in God's scalding light and strip to the white unshielded skin. *(Shivers slightly)* Then naked and cold, you say who you are and what your scared soul means in gorgeous sounds.

KERNEY

Write a new one for me.

John sits in silence a lengthening moment, then suddenly faces her.

JOHN

If I were to open my heart, we'd drown.

KERNEY

Is it that full?

JOHN

Oh no, plenty room. You're the one live person.

They face each other a long moment, to the point of unease.

John flinches first. He looks to his lap and tries to laugh.

KERNEY

You're a young man, Pa. I'm blocking your view.

JOHN

(Quietly) Never stop.

Kerney frowns in confusion.

John waves a hand dismissively.

Rescue—the sound of feet in the hall. They reach the open hall door, and Walter Parker knocks lightly on the door frame. Throughout, Walter enjoys alternating a refined white accent with his deeper native black; and though he sometimes parodies the stage "black servant," his self-assurance and dignity are strong. He also wears unusually stylish street clothes.

A large part of Kerney's enjoyment of his company lies in her ability to mimic him in the quick changes of dialect, rhythm and pitch.

WALTER

Hope I didn't break up no nice prayer meeting.

Kerney and John look up, smiling.

WALTER

(To Kerney) Like your dress. That new?

KERNEY

No, it's Lucille's—she and I swapped. I thought I'd try disguising myself.

WALTER

As poor Lucille? Shame *on* you, child. Lu can't see straight—that pitiful cock-eye, staring off sideways.

JOHN

(Restoring a more official tone) You turning in, Walter?

WALTER

No big hurry. I made that fifty pounds of chicken salad you said was so urgent.

JOHN

(To Kerney) Precisely one bowlful for Bailey—Biff is sick.

KERNEY

(Concerned) Of what?

WALTER

(Rushing in, gleeful) Stuck a dried navy bean way up through his nose, deep inside his brain.

JOHN

The bean was removed. End of saga please. But all Bailey's in-laws gathered prematurely and she's overwhelmed. I told her we'd help with the food at least.

KERNEY

Just so we don't see them.

JOHN

I pled the dysentery, you and me both.

WALTER

Kerney, how was your dance?

JOHN

Go on, Walter Parker. You turn white at midnight—I can't stand to watch.

WALTER

Just let me be polite to the lady. I asked her a question.

KERNEY

If you're staying up for news of that dance, drop down now and sleep. They had a colored band, thank God. Tank Thompson brought his pistol.

WALTER

Lord God, who's dead?

KERNEY

Nobody but the roof—three gaping holes. They rassled Tank down. All I know is, the girl he brought had passed out early on Purple Jesus—

JOHN

Purple *what?*

WALTER

Purple Jesus—nothing but grape juice and grain alcohol. You wouldn't like it.

JOHN

Nor none of my family, I hope.

WALTER

(To Kerney) So you went with Kip Patrick?

KERNEY

You know too much!

WALTER

Kip's a sport in *this* world! *(Waits)* Told me he loved you down to the ground.

JOHN

Walter Parker, go to bed.

WALTER

She needs to know this one last thing. Kip told me last Tuesday—I was getting the mail—he come up to me, right out of the sky, and said "Walter Parker, put in a good word. My heart's tore *up.*" Imagine my overwhelming surprise! I told him to hush—that I'd known you since before you were conscious, that you and I grew up together, and that he had a lot of changing to do before he could live anywhere near you.

KERNEY

You're fifteen years my senior, Walter. And don't you go telling Kip how to change.

WALTER

I know a thing or two about trifling white men—

Kerney suddenly stands.

Both men expect an outburst; but she throws up her arms to yawn, removes her shoes and goes to kiss her father good night.

She means to force Walter to leave at last.

WALTER

What time you all want breakfast tomorrow? I'm going to church.

JOHN

I'll be down at seven; got to work a few hours.

KERNEY

Kerney will see you when she sees you, Walter.

WALTER

All right. Say your prayers.

KERNEY

Same to you. By the way, you ain't said where *you* been tonight.

WALTER

Ain't going to neither! I respect your youth.

As Walter's steps recede, John and Kerney mime affectionate exhaustion.

KERNEY

How did we deserve him? He'd die for us.

JOHN

Or talk us to death, whichever came first. I'd die for him. Walter Parker is as fine a man as I ever knew—you name the color. I'd smite God's eyes if God tried to harm him.

KERNEY

You don't believe in God.

JOHN

I've said I wasn't on a first-name basis with whatever force made me and the stars.

KERNEY

That's clear as mud. *(Waits)* Steal a day off, tomorrow. Let's take a long ride.

JOHN

Sweetheart, court opens Monday morning. I've got a life to save—the Pemberton boy that sawed up his mother. Get Walter Parker to fix a picnic; you and Kip take the Buick.

KERNEY

(An unexaggerated demureness) Ladies don't make their own social plans.

JOHN

Kip is calling you night and day. All you got to do is answer.

KERNEY

Shall I marry him, Pa?

JOHN

Would you die for Kip?

KERNEY

(Incredulous) Sir?

JOHN

Do you truly *love* him? Love and death are the same kind of thing.

KERNEY

(Shakes her head, amazed) I may need a year or so to think *that* through.

JOHN

You got a good thinking place—your own quiet home. Far as I'm concerned, you can think fifty years.

KERNEY

You don't want that—me outliving you: a lone old lady locked up here blind.

JOHN

(Studies her a long moment) Some awful part of my heart does want it. *(Waits)* What's Walter Parker mean about Kip?

At last Kerney leans out far enough to touch her father. The fingers of her right hand cover his mouth.

John nods, then rises.

Kerney also rises, moves toward him, circles his waist and rests her head on his chest.

JOHN

You dying off?

KERNEY

(A hint of baby talk) Miss Bascomb is *whipped.*

JOHN

Shall I say "goo-goo," in my general policy of stunting your growth?

KERNEY

I wish I was.

JOHN

(Firmly) You wish you *were.* No such thing—you're as lovely a woman as I've ever known.

John stands another moment, then gently extricates himself, touches the crown of her head and steps back.

JOHN

It'll be daylight any minute now. You said you were whipped.

With that he begins to withdraw. By the end of the scene, he is out of sight.

KERNEY

I'm wide awake. *(Waits)* I never sat up with you asleep.

JOHN

I'm sure you'll be safe. Our safe little town—this is Eden, remember?

KERNEY

(Raising her voice) Am I Eve or the snake?

She stands another moment, then goes to a picture of her mother on the wall and touches the face. Then she darkens the room and leaves.

3

One-thirty, Sunday morning.

Kip enters the swept bare yard of a poor house. Though unpainted the house is in decent repair. There is the hint of light from an oil lamp at one window. Kip has taken a long ride and come here circuitously from Kerney. He has also drunk a good deal more gin and is high but not drunk. Unnerved then and near exhaustion, he heads straight for the door but suddenly pulls back and goes to the lighted window.

KIP

Ora—Ora Lee?

He backs off to a large white rock in front of the house and sits till he almost falls asleep.

In fact he does not hear Sarah Gaskin leave the house and walk toward him quickly. She is dressed in day clothes with a baby blanket around her shoulders.

Through the meeting, though they speak with rising force, they never harangue or abuse one another with voice or gesture. They have lived together, by day, for long years.

SARAH

Kipple Patrick, it's deep in the night.

KIP

I apologize, Sarah. You know who I want.

SARAH

Wanting ain't getting, everytime you whistle. All your life I drummed that in you.

KIP

You did and I'm grateful. Tonight's something special—the last time I'll do this.

SARAH

You been last-timing me and my family for some months now. Why you think we believe you tonight?

KIP

Don't make me say it.

SARAH

You got a new woman and ditched my child.

KIP

(Winces) That's putting it the meanest possible way.

SARAH

Feel meaner than that to Ora Lee.

KIP

Ora's always known—

SARAH

Because I *told* her. Then you were treating her open-handed and made her forget everything but you. I kept on warning; you kept on giving. So when you stopped coming round last month, Ora stopped eating. Every night when I got back from your daddy's, she'd meet me at the door. And I'd tell her the truth—you hadn't even breathed her name.

KIP

Have you told her why?

SARAH

I got a good big mirror your mama give me. Ora Lee spend hours a day staring at it. She know she's brown.

KIP

Sarah, do you blame me?

SARAH

Might as well blame a dead tree for lightning. From the day your mama died, I brought Ora with me right into your daddy's kitchen near you.

KIP

And she just got finer looking by the day.

SARAH

No more. She's thin as—

KIP

Wake her up please. I've truly got to tell her.

SARAH

(Studies Kip) Promise me one thing—you won't ever get near Ora again, not long as you live.

KIP

She's been too good to me too long.

SARAH

I stood by and watched the day you were born. I cooked nine-tenths of all the food ever crossed your lip, and you won't make me that easy promise? Man, how many women your body need?

KIP

It - is - not - that. Someway, I love her.

SARAH

And love Kerney Bascomb enough to promise her the rest of your days?

Sarah searches Kip's face, then steps back, turns and starts toward the house.

KIP

We all knew how the world was built, long before this started. I'll love Ora the rest of my life—you know I love *you*—but I love Kerney Bascomb enough to tell her I'd finish up here. *(Waits)* I'm sad as I know how to be and I'm sorry.

SARAH

Your *sorry* won't buy us a penny box of matches. I promised your mama to raise you up like you were mine, and I kept my promise—like you were some good and would live in the world to help me out, once *I* got helpless. What I feel in my heart now is liable to burn down this end of town and spread your way. You go home and sit up, waiting for fire.

Kip tries to laugh and break the tone.

KIP

I'll see you at breakfast. I'm going to church.

Sarah continues, silent, toward the house. Before she reaches the door, it opens.

Ora Lee stands in a long white nightgown, thrusting her arms into an ancient oversized sport jacket.

Sarah pushes in past her.

Ora runs out and stops short of Kip by several steps.

KIP

Thank the good Lord.

ORA

Hold your thanks till you see who I am.

KIP

I'd know you anywhere.

ORA

I don't know how. Seems like they used to call you Kipple Patrick.

KIP

(His liquor shows in a shaky bow) At your service.

ORA

I don't need nothing you selling or giving.

KIP

I hope to be buying.

ORA

God, strike him dumb! I never took a penny—

KIP

Just a good many greenbacks, three or four rings, a locket with a curl of your best friend's hair, a pretty wristwatch—right many nice gifts down through the sweet years.

ORA

That gin don't smell too sweet—Kerney Bascomb's gin.

The sound of Kerney's name shocks and confuses Kip. He responds with a harshness that, though unnatural, begins to show him the awfulness of his purpose here.

KIP

(Waits, grins) You put on some of your bleaching cream and go spying on the dance? Didn't see you there.

ORA

You ain't been seeing nothing dark as me these days.

KIP

My eyes can always find you.

Ora sees him at last with revulsion. She cannot speak yet but she mimes spitting at him.

KIP

(Laughs) You knew our game.

ORA

Game? What kind of game—you telling me all I hope to hear, through all these years? Then just because Jeffer Burns saw the light on that Bascomb bitch, you take your face right out of here. Well, keep it gone. I'm thriving, sucker.

KIP

(Stung but hiding it) I heard you were. Dave Robbins been seen riding out this way.

ORA

I been needing to tell you in person. Dave Robbins know the pathway to Paradise now.

KIP

Davey's all right, a safe old boy.

ORA

He take his time but he touch all bases.

KIP

(Laughs) Whoa! Still, Dave's not all that strong in the head. *(Taps his forehead)* Wrecks his car every week, bad judgment. *(Mock-whisper)* Small brain—

ORA

You the big brain, sure. Everybody know Kip's right most days. Hell, you could dress me, ride me to Raleigh to the Governor's Mansion, say I was yours—me and my brown butt—and the Governor's wife would shake my hand and set me down like an actual lady that she couldn't smell.

KIP

It'd be fun to try.

ORA

Some other year. Ora's tired this year. Needs to head back to sleep.

KIP

That pains me to hear.

ORA

It'll pain you a heap-damned-worse if I stay. I'm too naked though to be in the night and too tired of you.

Ora turns toward the house.

KIP

Want to take a short ride?

Ora continues walking till she reaches the porch steps.

ORA

(Mocking her own accent) I tell you what's the truth, white man—Ora Lee's night-riding days are past.

KIP

What about Dave Robbins, his big green roadster?

ORA

That's a whole nother business—Dave drives me in *daylight.*

She climbs the steps and stands on the stoop.

KIP

You going to say goodbye at least?

ORA

For a crisp new five-dollar bill, cash money.

KIP

Your words come high, lot higher than your—

ORA

Kipple, Kip—leave yourself *something* here.

KIP

Like what?

ORA

Not meanness, not trash.

Kip by now sees half the awfulness implicit in his being here at all, yet he cannot want to leave.

KIP

Could we start this over someway—do it right?

ORA

I didn't mean that. You too old, Kipple, to play this game. Too old and white—too white in the heart. God keeping score on your life now. Angels watching your hands.

Kip looks at both hands.

ORA

You go on home. *(Points)* That road yonder, right past Kerney Bascomb's. Don't blow no horn now and wake her up. She need all the beauty sleep she can get; might help her dry little titties grow.

KIP

(With controlled force) Keep that name out of your *mouth* forever.

ORA

(Smiles) My mouth ain't dirty—didn't used to be.

Kip shuts his eyes and waits to calm. But his bafflement rises.

He wipes his lips slowly with the back of a hand.

KIP

(Nods his head firmly) Filthy—tonight.

ORA

(Waits) Be nice now, son. Don't make bad blood. You be needing me—you and your poor daddy—when the nigger folk rise.

KIP

(Smiles) They all eating yeast?

ORA

Oh no. Eating knives. Eating cold wind and rain.

KIP

Remember me then. I'll lean on you.

ORA

Don't lean too hard; I might not know you. Might hand you over to the first hungry child.

KIP

Throw your mind back—four summers ago, way deep in the trees. First time you showed me all your sweetness.

ORA

Seem like I'm forgetting right much these days.

KIP

But work on it, Ora. Next time we'll find out what we got left.

ORA

Next time I'll be too bright for you to see. I'm getting more splendid by the night now, boy. Be good to your eyes; don't glance at Ora—her and her son and all her kin. She'll blind you fast.

She launches a final dazzling smile, then slowly goes in.

Kip stands a moment, fixing the memory.

Then he shakes his head in confusion and leaves.

4

A half hour later. The Bascomb house is still bathed in moonlight. Kerney's bedroom is on the ground floor with a single long half-open window.

The sound of a car door gently shut.

Kip enters, smoothing his hair and clothes (no tie, open shirt).

He goes to the center and cups his hands to call for Kerney, then changes his mind.

He lays his seersucker jacket on the ground and goes toward the window.

Quietly he begins to sing "Jeannie with the Light Brown Hair."

He lifts his hands in almost mock-prayer—the gin is still in him.

Then he pushes the window wider open.

After a long wait Kerney appears, full-length in the window. She wears a long nightgown but seems wide awake.

It takes her awhile to notice Kip.

KERNEY

Go *on*—

KIP

Where?

KERNEY

Fly, to the stars—I know you can.

KIP

Girl, are you still drunk?

KERNEY

I never was but I know who is.

KIP

Come save me then.

KERNEY

I'm no missionary. Save your own soul.

KIP

My body's the problem.

KERNEY

I thought you'd have that cooled down by now.

KIP

No ma'm, still steaming. I've been out seeing to the orders you gave me.

KERNEY

Pa and Walter Parker are asleep. You ought to be.

KIP

(Holds up his arms for her to join him) One short look—at just your face—and then I'll fly.

Kerney thinks, then slowly climbs through her window, crouches on the ledge and—almost dizzy—sits there.

KERNEY

You'll kill me yet.

Kip stays in place.

KIP

That's not my intention.

KERNEY

What is?

Kip studies her slowly, hoping to calm the sadness from Ora.

KIP

Watching you, all dazed and helpless.

KERNEY

Get one thing into your dazed head—Kerney's as helpless as a Mexican rattlesnake.

She springs from the window ledge to the ground and approaches Kip.

KERNEY

What did you tell her? *(When Kip looks puzzled)* You said you obeyed some orders of mine.

KIP

The way's clear now.

KERNEY

What did you tell her?

KIP

I'm not here begging for *your* secrets, notice.

KERNEY

(Waits) Your concubine was never a secret.

KIP

That's a scandalous lie.

KERNEY

I've known it forever. So have Pa and Walter Parker. And all my friends. So's every colored person between here and Raleigh.

KIP

We won't get anywhere, telling lies. I came here to tell you I did what you asked. Think it over in your spare time, hear?

KERNEY

(Studies him slowly, nods) Now go on to bed.

She moves toward her window.

For a moment Kip balks, stunned by her apparent refusal in the face of his news. But then as she reaches to climb back in, he takes her arm.

She pulls free and stays by the window.

Again Kip is won by her presence and tries to raise the tone.

KIP

Those Mexican rattlers you spoke about? They look right fine, undressed for bed.

KERNEY

You don't want to corner one.

KIP

You never hurt a gnat. *(Studies her again)* You need me, girl.

KERNEY

You'd make a nice hat rack to stand in the hall.

KIP

You'd make a fine statue for the Temple of Venus.

KERNEY

(Takes a step toward him) I'll make you a practical proposition, son. Get somebody sober to drive you to Raleigh. Find you an artist and I'll pose for him, long as it takes to make you a perfect life-sized *me*—real hair, china teeth: your own Kerney Bascomb. Then tease her, squeeze her, do anything you need to that I don't have to watch. *(Turns to her window)*

Kip's head has begun to clear. His voice is firm.

KIP

This is so damned childish. I beg your pardon.

KERNEY

I can sleep tomorrow. I'm not as accustomed to gin as you and I'm—

KIP

We're both heading south.

KERNEY

With the wild geese or what?

KIP

With the man you'll spend your grown life beside.

Kerney moves closer to see his eyes. Then she steps well back.

KERNEY

I'm no orphan dog. I don't follow strangers.

KIP

You've known me most of the days of your life. I'm your heart's own choice.

KERNEY

(Laughs one note) Brace yourself, boy. *(Waits)* My heart hasn't chose.

Kip approaches and reaches for her hand.

Kerney draws back.

KERNEY

I'm thinking. But I have not chosen. I've got real duties—I'm all Pa's got.

KIP

He's got his *life*—his law practice, this house for a home. He's got Walter Parker.

KERNEY

If I leave now he'll howl like the wind through a burnt-out barn.

KIP

Brace yourself now: that's - the - way - life - is. You *want* to leave here. You said you were trapped.

KERNEY

It's the trap I *know*—no mean dark corners.

KIP

If it's my dark corner you're worried about, I told you that's gone.

This late, and near her father's window, Kerney will not deal with the subject of Ora. She shakes her head No.

KIP

(A new calm tack) I know for a fact that your father wants you to have a grown life. *(Waits)* I asked him.

KERNEY

Don't start a clean day with a lie, Kip Patrick.

KIP

(Raising his hand to swear) Two whole days ago, in his office. I'd gone in to ask him about a land problem, my family's land. And when we were finished, your father sat back and asked a few questions about my life—any hopes I had. I didn't feel like he was fishing hard, but finally the trust in his face made me tell him. I said "Mr. Bascomb, I'm in love with Kerney."

KERNEY

No wonder he was so blue tonight.

KIP

Blue? No, lord, he was pink with joy. He said "She mentions your name more than seldom." Then we sang your praises in all major keys.

KERNEY

How sad for you both.

KIP

No! By the end we were whooping like monkeys. *(When he sees a sign of anger in Kerney)* Whooping in *love*, child—pure brotherly love. He told me about you before I knew you—how you set fire to your grandaddy's hair, how you lamed the gray horse, how you took the good rolling pin and squashed your goldfish.

KERNEY

To see how they worked. But you never got serious with him again?

KIP

Sorry. I told him he couldn't change my heart, no matter what terrors he dredged from the past.

Kerney moves quickly to the edge of dark—her back to Kip, facing the audience. This is hard to hear.

KIP

Then he finally gave me a reason to hope.

Kerney crouches to the ground and covers her ears.

KIP

He said "I'll give her to the man she chooses, no sooner than that." I said "Will you bless him?" He walked all the long way back to his desk. Then he faced me and nodded "It'll be God's will."

KERNEY

(Faces Kip, stands) That proves you're lying. Pa's an old agnostic.

KIP

(Smiles) Ah! I too smelled a lawyer's trick. I said "Sir, you're no church-going man." He said "True, Kipple, but that's owing to the scenery: those ladies' hats, those fat preachers stuffed down in swallow-tailed coats."

KERNEY

(Nods) His voice.

Disheartened, she moves a little farther from Kip.

KIP

Marry me.

KERNEY

Why?

KIP

(With smiling impatience) I've done the last big deed you demanded. You're changing ground fast as a Mexican rattler.

KERNEY

(Waits) I need to know what drives a person as smart as you to give up freedom and all his sins and crave wild me.

KIP

(Waits) You know about the beauty part, but there's so much more. *(Tries to see her in the dark)* —How scary you are, what a daring soul. Everybody else we know is groggy. I've been a stunt pilot all my life and so have you. I need a brave wife.

KERNEY

I'm weak as water.

KIP

You're a damned *power* plant. You glow in the dark. You'd gnaw your arm off, neat at the shoulder, if you got caught. You've got a mind in all that hair, that glorious hair—

KERNEY

Just stay out of the beauty department.

KIP

I can see children all in your eyes, all lovely as you—

KERNEY

No healthy young man ever wants children. Tell that to some sucker-homebody, not wise old Kerney.

KIP

(Waits, then with new firmness) All right, goddammit—I feel like I'm strong and need to bear weight. You're what I want to lift

and carry. I want to bear you forward through life, whatever years are left.

As Kip's explanation grew, it gradually fascinated Kerney with its passion; and eventually it touched her. She moves back nearer, into the moonlight.

KERNEY

All this moonlight and all that honor—Kip, I think you mean it. And a lot of the time, I want to step toward you. But there's still big trouble, deep back in my head. *(Waits)* I'm such a part of my father's life, so maybe I've had all the marriage I need. More likely though, I don't have the talent. I just can't say, tonight or next week, where I'm likely to be six minutes from now, much less sixty years.

KIP

Do you love me?

KERNEY

Now you sound like Jeffer.

Kip turns and begins to leave.

KERNEY

I may well need you someday soon. *(When he stops to listen)* But maybe right now, here tonight, it's your age that's the problem. Your glands and all—

KIP

(Calm but strong) My glands cranked up more than eight years ago. By now I've learned how to screen glands out of my hopes and dreams.

KERNEY

(Nods, in innocence) I'll try to answer you soon as I can. Right now my tired runaway mind wants to stand in a field, with shade and a pear tree and no - other - thing.

KIP

You scare me.

KERNEY

I told you I would. I scare myself so bad I can't breathe.

KIP

(Believing her, relenting a little) I've told you my feelings. I won't try again. Remember my question—will you stay by me, through whatever comes, till you or I end? Like it or not, we were both born with faces people fly up against like moths to a light—

KERNEY

Or me to the moon.

Through the following Kip slowly walks over and stands close to Kerney.

KIP

So nobody's going to leave us alone. If we don't choose each other soon, we'll be worn down with people coming at us. That's not pride; it's a flat damned fact.

He takes Kerney's hands.

Suddenly she raises the joined hands and kisses each, entirely sincere.

Kip is moved but after a moment he withdraws both hands and steps back.

KERNEY

Soon, soon. You've got my word.

Kip turns and walks away slowly.

As he sinks into darkness, Kerney can't help teasing.

KERNEY

Take several more words—all my favorites. Take— *(Waits, then with hushed but exaggerated relish)* Alabaster. Camomile. Resurrection. Take *cellar door.*

KIP

(At a distance) Get serious; that's two.

Kerney reaches for her window ledge.

KERNEY

Take *forsaking all others.*

KIP

Take *hush your mouth.*

At the sound of Kip's car, Kerney waves once.

Then she makes the small leap and enters her window.

5

Twenty minutes later. The backyard of the Patrick house—Kip's birthplace and home.

The sounds of Kip stabling his car for the night.

Frank Patrick, Kip's father, is sitting on the porch in a rocking chair. He wears pajamas and a cotton bathrobe.

Kip appears, pauses in the yard for a last look at the setting moon, then smooths his hair and clothes to enter the house. He barely touches the bottom step of the dark porch.

FRANK

Don't wake your old father.

KIP

Doesn't anybody in the *state* ever sleep at night?

FRANK

You making a scientific study?

KIP

No sir, hoping for peace. Since dusk, everybody's been piling burdens on me.

FRANK

Well, don't go in yet. The house is still hot.

Kip sits on the steps below his father's chair.

KIP

The local climate is the least of my cares.

FRANK

What's the most? Want to tell your pro - gen - i - tor?

KIP

(Exhausted) Take a quick guess.

FRANK

(Waits) The girl turned you down.

KIP

You're wrong both ways—she's way past a *girl*, and she hasn't said *nothing*.

FRANK

(Waits again) Kerney's really your pick? You can have it, you know—any girl your age in this wide county and half the widows.

KIP

You've made extensive inquiries, in the woods?

FRANK

I've watched quite a few pairs of female eyes. You draw notice, Kip. Love seeks you, boy.

KIP

It's late but I hear you saying I'm cursed.

FRANK

That's a dark way to put it.

KIP

I've known my share of dark.

FRANK

(A finger to his lips) Tell the gods you never said it, or they'll send a fresh disaster by morning—a corpse in the cereal, an eye in the milk.

KIP

We lost our mothers too young, Kerney and I.

He turns to face his father; and through what follows, Kip sits, stands, roams the yard and returns.

KIP

The way I see it, it makes you doubt love—forever after. A human mother is the one live creature that's guaranteed to love you just because you're alive.

FRANK

Are fathers so hateful?

KIP

I'm not blaming you. I'm trying to help my pitiful brain understand Kerney Bascomb—she shunts back and forth from me to the moon. See, Mother lived till I was fourteen. Kerney could barely read when hers died, so how can I expect her to know that love's as likely on Earth as hate?

FRANK

Kerney was up around ten or eleven when her mother died. She ought to know.

KIP

(Rubs his tired eyes) It's too late to argue. She mistrusts me, bad. *(Waits and then, in his father's silence)* You lost interest in me?

FRANK

Never that. I was just struck dumb. I thought I heard you crack the lock on a barred door.

KIP

It's an ugly sight.

FRANK

I saw trench war and mustard gas.

KIP

Tonight I outright proposed to Kerney. We'd tear off tonight to South Carolina and be back here in three or four days.

FRANK

A sensible offer.

KIP

(Meets Frank's eyes) She balked at Ora. I must get rid of Ora.

FRANK

(Firmly) Rid? Get *rid?* Is Ora some vermin you crush with a foot?

KIP

You know what she meant.

FRANK

Go blind yourself then; put both eyes out. In this small town, you're bound to see Ora. *(Now Kip is silent)* May I ask a question?

KIP

You know this hurts like eating barbed wire.

FRANK

You haven't shocked me. But two questions please.

Kip waits, then nods.

FRANK

Is Ora's little boy your son? And does Ora still want you?

KIP

She says the boy is not mine, no. And no sir, she spat on me tonight. You're right though—let me see Ora's face; and I want all of her, God knows I do.

FRANK

God won't hear that as calmly as me. Of course you want her. If I were your age, I'd have locked her upstairs here.

KIP

You respected Mother.

FRANK

When I was your age, I wasn't married either. I reeked like a damned polecat with musk.

KIP

And you had a girl?

FRANK

Not colored—poor white. Her pa and brothers were the worst grade of trash, but damned if she didn't milk my heart dry for five years. I hurt by the minute, like you hurt now. But I craved every cell of her skin right on.

KIP

And after you married, you still saw her?

FRANK

I see her now, in town every Saturday. But I stopped touching her a month before my wedding—*I* stopped; she was howling for us to keep on.

KIP

Must I stop dead?

FRANK

Kerney demands it. I suspect God does.

KIP

No decent way to see Ora Lee, say, every few weeks and still be married?

FRANK

Not on this planet, no. Honor Kerney or quit.

KIP

Do *you* care, either way?

FRANK

Tune your ears up, son. *(Waits)* Maybe it's all my years of teaching Latin—Cicero, Seneca, thoughts on slavery. But surely, I hope you can let Ora go. Thank her kindly; give her some nice gift, some money for the boy. But let her know—and pound it in your skull—that, far as you're concerned, Ora is gone.

Kip is clearly pained and confused.

KIP

Let's rest all that.

FRANK

It won't rest, son.

KIP

I mean I'm sick of all my woes. I ought to just be the first Methodist monk. *(When Frank is silent)* Tell me how you've lived, with just me here—you've looked so fine.

FRANK

(Laughs once) I felt like the bear that failed dancing class.

KIP

You paid Sarah to keep me clean. And you stood close, to teach me duty.

FRANK

I was raised by a woman, like most human beings. That tends to teach kindness—or used to at least. Raising you right was all I knew.

KIP

And now I bring you this ugly mess. There must have been times—maybe now, God knows—when you wanted to run.

FRANK

(Faces Kip, firmly) Or put a cold pistol to my temple and fired.

KIP

Have I made it that bad?

FRANK

You truly don't know?

KIP

I may. But tell me.

FRANK

You were maybe sixteen and had gone to church. You well know church was never my style; but that one morning, I had a revelation. I was upstairs, grading a set of the worst Latin tests a teacher ever got. I put down the last failing grade and said "I have ruined this too." I'd really felt drawn to teach other humans the joy I know, just standing in the shade of Virgil and Horace. But now I'd ruined those children's chance. I could hear Sarah downstairs, rolling out biscuits. Then plain as day I saw you growing up, tall and straight, with just good Sarah and me underground. I took my pistol, walked to the bathroom and sat on the tub. I thought I'd recite a poem first, and I got as far as the second line of Hadrian's epitaph—"Animula vagula blandula." Then I heard your strong feet climb the stairs. You called out "Father"—

KIP

And you didn't answer.

FRANK

Remember what you said?

KIP

(Waits) At least I remember finding you there. *(Hunts for the words)* I told you the text of the sermon I'd heard.

FRANK

It saved my life.

KIP

(Waits again) "My grace is sufficient for thee"—what Christ tells Paul, when Paul despairs.

FRANK

I looked up the Greek. It means something like "What I give you is enough." Thank you, son—kindly.

KIP

You don't believe the Bible.

FRANK

I'm thanking you for the gifts you give. They were real that day; they're real tonight.

KIP

(Yawns) So's Heaven and you don't even want to go.

FRANK

If it's there at the last minute, smuggle me in.

KIP

Me? Lord, Father. Lean somewhere else.

FRANK

(Laughs once) God loves you.

KIP

(Shakes his head) Poor God.

Kip leans back and shuts his eyes.

Frank stands and turns to go inside.

6

A few minutes later. The Bascomb and Patrick houses are visible in the darkness.

Kip still sleeps in the chair on his porch; Kerney, in her nightgown, is in her own bed.

Dimly we also see John Bascomb and Frank Patrick asleep in their beds.

A high uncanny music begins; and the general darkness is broken by a rise of strange light, a low internal glow as if blossoming from the room itself—first, in Kerney's room as her dream begins and then, as her dream flows into Kip's dream, on him.

Seated on the foot of Kerney's bed, fully dressed in a good white dress and gloves of the late 1920s, is Christine, Kerney's mother, who died eleven years ago. Christine takes no special notice of her sleeping daughter but rises, slowly walks to a chest of drawers and begins to search the folded clothing—a blouse, a handkerchief, a summer skirt. Her concern rises as she unfolds and rejects the sparse trousseau. Depending upon the resources of individual stages, Christine may mime her worry by conducting a dignified, but not hectic, search of a half-empty closet or wardrobe. The point is that Christine has been permitted to return, this once, for her daughter's wedding but is distraught to find such a lack of appropriate clothing.

The sleeping Kerney responds to her dream with restrained movements in bed and occasional restrained sounds.

Once Christine has established the lack, she stands in the center of the room to form her plan. When she has it, she looks down at Kerney. Then she moves close enough to extend a hand to touch her. But the touch just misses connection, and Christine does not try again.

She silently passes through the house, not pausing at the room where John sleeps. And she quickly enters the space between the Bascomb and Patrick houses.

At the start of the dream, Ora Lee also came out of her house, handsomely dressed in violet purple with a matching flower tucked in her hair. As the two mothers meet and search, Ora walks to the absolute center of the space and sits on the white rock.

Christine seems not to see her.

But from the moment Christine passes, Ora watches her intently, apparently able to see through the walls of the Patrick house.

As Christine enters, the glow rises on Kip where he sits, dressed but unconscious.

There his mother—Dorothy Patrick—sits in a straight chair, awake but motionless. She also is dressed in old formal white with white gloves. When Christine enters Kip's doorway, Dorothy looks up in surprise. She and Christine were intimate friends and have not met since their deaths.

As she gradually recognizes her friend, Christine stands with open arms to embrace her. They remain together for a moment, miming their affection by examining details of their dress and jewelry. Then Dorothy points to Kip fondly and takes Christine's hand to touch his hair.

At that moment a rise of light on Kip suggests that Kerney's dream has now entered Kip's head. From here on, both Kip and Kerney share the dream in their separate beds.

Without further communication Christine and Dorothy go together to another room, the one in which Frank sleeps unnoticed. Dorothy opens a drawer and removes a stack of clothing.

Christine is surprised and puzzled.

But Dorothy leads the way outdoors; and there in the space between the two houses, they sort the stack—a white negligee, white silk stockings and a wedding veil. Both women are content and Christine is greatly eased. They refold the clothes and together bear them silently out. When they reach the white rock, they stop in front of Ora. With no suggestion of taunting, each of them unfolds a piece of the trousseau and shows it to Ora—the white negligee and the veil.

Ora takes a long moment to study the veil. Then she leans slightly forward and touches it.

They give her a moment to feel the cloth, then they gently take the veil from her hands.

Ora never smiles but she shows no reluctance to give it up.

As the mothers enter Kerney's house, the lights on both the white houses begin to fade. But Ora stays on in a central glow.

As both dreams end Ora remains on her white rock, bright and unbowed, facing outward. The light on her begins to brighten, then a sudden blackout.

It is vital to the seriousness of the dream that none of the women's poses or gestures is exaggerated into a parody of silent-film action. They are players in Kerney's crucial dream, an event that profoundly shapes her final decision. So they move with composure, conscious of their importance but in no way comic. In brief they are their old selves still, possessed only of a mild new radiance and slowed a little as if moving in cold oil.

ACT TWO

1

Sunday morning, ten o'clock.

In the Bascomb kitchen, Walter Parker stands at the stove, cooking and humming a gospel hymn. A table in the midst of the room is set for one.

Kerney appears at the hall doorway in nightgown and robe. Her hair is uncombed but her face is clean.

She clears her throat.

Throughout, Walter Parker rings swift changes, from genuine feeling to more than half-conscious parody of "black servant" manners.

WALTER

(Caught off guard, jumps) Don't *do* that, Kerney, else you'll have an ice-cold cook on your plate instead of my beautiful eggs.

KERNEY

Not for me.

WALTER

Oh *yes.* You're seasick, child. Got to eat grease to press that gin on out of your soul.

Kerney moves into the room and sits at the table, though not at the set place.

KERNEY

What makes you an expert on seasickness?

WALTER

Ain't I been in the U.S. Navy? Ain't I been to Spain and Gibraltar? I seen a lot more than you—that is, up to now.

KERNEY

And what happens now?

WALTER

You, big lady—you getting so rich, on Patrick money. We'll all be flashing gold teeth by Christmas.

KERNEY

What possessed you to think the Patricks are rich?

WALTER

(Taps his skull) My beautiful brain, best spy in town.

KERNEY

Tell me what it knows.

WALTER

You'd say I'm lying and go your way.

KERNEY

This morning I need you. *(When Walter mimes amazement)* I had a bad dream.

WALTER

You come to the dream man.

KERNEY

Mother was here, early this morning—seemed real as me. And she seemed all right, so why was it bad?

WALTER

(Calmly, in earnest) It wasn't, far from it. You were just surprised. See, the weekends are when most spirits travel. So from Friday to Sunday, I sprinkle a line of sulfur on my doorsill. An evil spirit won't step over sulfur. Good spirits pass right through and do their blessings.

Kerney is more interested than usual in Walter's claims.

He sees it and rushes on.

WALTER

Last night, right here, something scattered my sulfur.

KERNEY

A hungry mouse.

WALTER

No mouse *that* big. Bound to been your mother, if you seen her too. She must have checked in to watch me breathing—spirits don't understand we still have to breathe. *(Waits)* Why would she need to see you last night?

KERNEY

Pick a reason; you know all my secrets.

WALTER

(Nods) Hurts my *mind*, hiding your mess from poor Mr. John—all that canoodling with the Burns boy and Kip. Mr. John thinks you're pure as the driven snow.

KERNEY

Remember Mae West? *(Her Westian voice again)* "I used to be Snow White but I drifted." *(But when Walter only shakes his head, her own face clouds)* I think my mother wants me to get married.

WALTER

That's the story then. You can't disobey.

KERNEY

Why not? I'm old enough to choose.

WALTER

You're sitting here, on Sunday morning, defying as good a soul as your mother when she took the pain to trudge back here and guide you right?

KERNEY

Why did it pain her?

WALTER

You don't think leaving God in Heaven and struggling back here is some kind of pain? Well, don't worry—you won't never get the chance. *(When Kerney takes him seriously)* You still haven't told me what she said.

KERNEY

I don't think she spoke. *(Waits)* It's already fading, just now as we talk.

WALTER

Daylight's hard on dreams. I write every one of mine down in the dark.

He brings a full plate of eggs and toast to Kerney.

She reaches for a knife and fork; and through the rest of their talk, she eats every morsel.

KERNEY

Her main point seemed to be my clothes—I didn't have a trousseau.

WALTER

Trousseau! You ain't got *fieldhand* clothes. It's a public sin to make other people even look at clothes as trashy as yours.

KERNEY

I reach for a new dress, and then I think "This would feed twelve Chinese children all year."

WALTER

The way you look'd scare those Chinese children so bad they not even hungry. Kerney, you getting married in the fall. And fall clothes are coming in the store every day.

KERNEY

Who said anything about next fall?

WALTER

You ain't planning to marry in this heat? Honeymoon in August? Child, you'll still be a virgin at Christmas!

KERNEY

(Laughing but half-earnest) Show some respect!

WALTER

I show every color of human being just what they earn. You act like a lady, I'll bow when you pass.

KERNEY

Calm, Walter, calm. *(Waits)* It sounds like you heard Kip's proposal last night.

WALTER

(A momentary Buddha imitation) I know what I know. *(Waits)* You ought to said Yes.

KERNEY

And elope last night and leave Pa wondering if I was dead?

WALTER

Writing *has* been invented. Leave him a note. *(When Kerney begins to scribble with a finger on the bare tabletop)* Listen to your dreams, child. Your mother said *church.*

KERNEY

How?

WALTER

You mentioned a trousseau. Name me the fool that buys her a trousseau and then elopes. *(Pats his own back)*

KERNEY

(Taking him seriously again) How much you know about Ora Lee Gaskin?

WALTER

Mrs. *Roosevelt* knows about Ora Lee. She's public news—with that son so white he nearly got pink eyes.

KERNEY

Is he Kip's son?

WALTER

Somebody white had more than a *hand* in making that child.

(Waits) Fine little boy, talked to him yesterday up by the courthouse. He—

KERNEY

I lowered the boom.

WALTER

(Smiling at first, then earnest) Lord, here come the boom! Let me guess. You ruled Ora out. *(When Kerney nods)* Now that child'll starve.

KERNEY

(Genuinely disturbed) Ora can work. Sarah works—

WALTER

It's not your worry.

KERNEY

You scared me though.

WALTER

I'll scare you a heap more, now that you're grown.

KERNEY

It's *all* scary, Walter. Why else am I stalling?

WALTER

Nobody can stall; it just comes and finds you. Heap worse if it catch you at home by yourself, nobody to hold you. Get on out of this house into daylight, meet some kind people, let yourself laugh some and sleep peaceful nights. Why else your mama come here last night?—to tell you *that*.

KERNEY

(Waits) You're single as me. And you look happy.

WALTER

Walter Parker's life is banned in Boston! But yes, I've had a fat piece of fun and I'm hunting more. Your dream got other plans for you.

KERNEY

(Straight at him) If there's justice in Heaven, we'll be brother and sister.

WALTER

Hold on; you moving faster than God. This white-and-black-*together* stuff is nothing much better than "nigger secrets"—the stuff white men tell us, just to talk: how much liquor their wife knocks back, what high-yaller gal the preacher is bumping.

KERNEY

I almost mentioned Ora to Pa—last night—but then you walked in and stopped me.

WALTER

(Gazing to Heaven) Thank you, Jesus. *(Then to Kerney)* You don't think a lawyer in a one-horse town knows about Kip and Ora? *(When Kerney is plainly waiting for more)* Don't make him tell you what he sees in the dark. This is your life now—he won't in your dream.

KERNEY

(Eager) He was—but asleep.

WALTER

Exactly. Now if you mean to leave, leave fast and sharp—in the night, just a kind note propped on this table.

KERNEY

(Nods, waits) Or this—I leave here tonight, by myself. I take a train to Raleigh—or Piss Ant, Georgia. I get me a room with a clean widow-lady. Then I get me a job—

WALTER

What as?

KERNEY

I could be a secretary. I could be—

WALTER

You could be flat dead in the street. You can't spell *cat*, much less type. You got one thing exactly you can sell, and the whole world can spell it.

KERNEY

Be ashamed!

WALTER

God's truth. If you leave here alone, you'll starve by Thursday or sell your skin.

KERNEY

I'm smart. I could be a companion to a rich old lady that wanted to travel.

WALTER

Or a bad old man that meant to stay home. You listen to Walter one more time. You sit safe here till you know what your mother meant last night.

KERNEY

If I go with Kip, I'll know all the answers?

WALTER

Not a chance in the world—*Kip* don't know the answers. Anything can happen to anybody anytime.

KERNEY

What a way to think!

WALTER

Only right way; every black person know it. But Kerney, *go on.* It's every bit scary as a cold cyclone. Still your dream says go - on - off. Take Kip's hand, in church or out. That's your best ticket out of here.

KERNEY

(Smiles) So you'll have room for *your* butt to grow?

WALTER

My butt is content.

KERNEY

You could truck up to Philly and be a free man—sit by white folks on the bus, eat with white folks in every café.

WALTER

And starve in the street in a heap colder weather than we got down here. I know people here.

KERNEY

In Latin class, ten times a week, Kip's father would point to some Roman saying one big thing, "*Stay where you're cherished.*"

WALTER

Your father is way too easy to cherish. You may need to run out of here, just to leave.

KERNEY

But aside from the dream, why with Kip?

WALTER

Cause he's somebody loves you that's not your own blood, not crazy, not mean. He got a good job in your home town, stands neat in his clothes, keeps his hair lying down.

KERNEY

(Waits) Walter, Ora was in that dream.

WALTER

But *leaving*, am I right? Ora was leaving? *(When Kerney nods)* Kip Patrick knows when it's time to get grown.

KERNEY

I guess I hope so.

Each sits quietly, calming the air.

The sounds of mounting heat rise in volume—crickets, birds.

WALTER

(Quietly) Is your mother all right?

KERNEY

(Nods) Gained a nice lot of weight. Almost like a girl—

WALTER

I knew Miss Christine had earned her bliss. *(Waits)* I held her the instant she left this world.

KERNEY

Pa never told me.

WALTER

Mr. John was downtown, getting her pills.

KERNEY

Was it that hard to watch?

WALTER

Oh no, girl, no. Right at the end her face got young. She said "Walter Parker, here, set me up." Your pa had told me not to move her an inch; it hurt her that bad. So I told her I couldn't, and she warned me hard. *(Walter's voice lightens but no falsetto)* "If you don't sit me up this instant, I'll claw my way back here from the grave and press you *down.*"

So I raised her up. Turned out, that way she could finally breathe. She drew one breath about two minutes long and shot me a smile. Then she said "Walter Parker, give that frown a rest. I'm looking at things you can't even dream. Where I am now is all pure water with low trees smelling like white honeysuckle. Tell everybody I know, the grass is deep."

I said "Miss Christine, then you mow it for me"—she knew how much I hate to mow grass. She opened her mouth to say her answer. I could see she meant it to be another joke. The air moved in front of her face but no words came.

KERNEY

Nothing about her orphan daughter?

WALTER

Sorry, no ma'm. She had moved on from you. *(Searches Kerney's face)* You wouldn't want me to make up a lie?

KERNEY

God no. That's the best news I ever heard in my life. *(Waits)* It lets me stand up now and dress—

WALTER

And leave out of here?

KERNEY

(Smiles) Let me get clean first. My head wants to go, but my heart's reared way back.

WALTER

Your heart's outvoted, two to one—me and your mother. *(When Kerney shakes her head)* Trouble with you, from the cradle up, is—when you need to jump, you pull back and *think*. *(Demonstrates)* Clamp your nose in your fingers, shut your eyes and *jump*.

KERNEY

(Smiles) I wish I could see this as, someway, funny like everybody else. Right now though it's late, and my limbs need bathing.

She pinches her nose as if at a stench.

Walter follows suit as Kerney leaves. Then he slowly gathers the dishes.

2

Twelve-fifteen.

Kip—in a fresh summer suit—returns from church. On the porch he hangs his jacket on the back of a rocking chair, loosens his tie, sits and begins to study the church bulletin.

Soon Sarah Gaskin appears behind the screen door. She wears a typical maid's uniform of the time—a starched cotton dress in royal blue with white collar, white cuffs on the short sleeves and white buttons. Throughout, she is plainly heavy with memory of the previous night and is in no mood to humor Kip.

SARAH

How was it?

KIP

Church? Well, the music was weird. *(Turns back to reading)*

SARAH

Some lady was singing?

KIP

(Preoccupied) You know those voices that sing in the cracks *between* the notes, and soon the fillings in your teeth start humming?

SARAH

I don't let myself get caught when a white lady sings.

Still sore from his meeting with Sarah last night, Kip continues trying to ignore her presence.

Sarah turns to walk away but reconsiders, opens the screen, walks toward Kip and hands him a small draw-strung bag.

SARAH

While Mr. Frank is taking his walk—

Kip takes the bag, feels it carefully and sets it on the floor beside him.

KIP

How much of this was your idea?

SARAH

(Firm but low, throughout) Not a piece of it, Kip.

KIP

I'd never have known her if she wasn't your child.

SARAH

Don't go laying your meanness on me. You knocked Ora Lee down *low* last night. She fool enough to stand still and take your mess. I don't have that kind of time on my hands. I been too busy, raising you since your mother died; trying to make you somebody decent. *(Turns to the door)* Ora told me to get a receipt.

KIP

(Incredulous) In writing?

SARAH

Ora don't want you claiming she owe you one red cent.

Kip shakes the contents of the bag into his hand, studies the few small objects and begins to replace them.

KIP

(Facing Sarah) I don't see the boy.

SARAH

Not going to neither.

KIP

You know who fathered that child.

SARAH

Any four men might have a piece of that child—two of em was white.

KIP

When that child was born, Ora Lee was aimed at *me.*

SARAH

You think what you need to. I think what's true.

KIP

You can look at his eyes and not see me?

SARAH

I seen you ninety-eight percent of the days of your life; and Kipple, you ain't nowhere to be seen in nothing he got. He a kind little fellow, peaceful manners.

Kip reaches behind him to pocket the bag.

KIP

Will she hate me for good?

SARAH

Sat up rocking her body all night and cutting your picture in ten thousand pieces.

KIP

Did the boy understand?

SARAH

He got a name—say it.

KIP

Lawrence *(Waits)* —Gaskin? Is that his last name?

SARAH

(Nods) My name, his mother's. No, any kind of meanness put Lawrence to sleep.

KIP

If I give you pieces of money through the years, will you see he gets it—for clothes and school?

SARAH

Kip, get my family out - of - your - mind. I never wanted any of us to be there.

KIP

You brought Ora into this kitchen.

SARAH

Can't a poor woman nurse her clean polite daughter and not draw hornets on her from the sky?

KIP

(Waits) If I get to Heaven and you're up there, will you let me win a round every thousand years?

SARAH

(Unsmiling) I'll be there. You worry about you.

Frank enters from his walk and stands at the bottom of the steps.

KIP

See anything good?

FRANK

Saw a squirrel miss his footing and fall fifty yards. When he saw me watching, he cut his eyes at me with a sick little grin as if to say "I *planned* that. Hope it looked as good as it felt." *(Waits)* Hear anything that instructive in church?

KIP

(Smiles) Afraid not, no. I just stared at my soul.

FRANK

(Still in the yard) That explain the dark scowl?

KIP

(Faces his father, unsmiling, and nods) Sarah, what's on the stove?

SARAH

Pork roast, mashed potatoes, corn pudding, string beans, field peas, sliced tomatoes, celery and biscuits.

FRANK

That all?

SARAH

(Still serious) Lemon pie with my good meringue.

KIP

God forbid we should eat bad meringue. *(Checks his watch)* What time?

SARAH

Same time every Sunday of your long life.

Sarah opens the screen and silently enters.

KIP

(Calls after her) Thank you though, hear?

FRANK

What's she done now?

KIP

Tried to save my soul for the ten millionth time. You don't want details. *(Checks his watch again and half-rises)*

FRANK

If I sit down a minute, can we still converse?

KIP

When did we stop?

FRANK

I thought last night might have finished us both.

As Frank begins to climb the steps, Kip stands, takes his jacket, passes his father and walks to the edge of the yard.

KIP

We've got our lives to talk in, Father. I've got a short mission.

FRANK

Any way I can help?

KIP

(Turns to leave) You already did, late last night.

FRANK

(Lowers his voice) Ora Lee?

Kip nods.

FRANK

(Sits slowly) That's a story worth ending, the best you can.

Kip nods and leaves.

Frank watches him go, then loosens his tie and prepares to nap.

3

A quarter-hour later.

Kip climbs the steps of Sarah's house and knocks once. No answer. He knocks again louder.

KIP

Ora Lee. Please. *(More silence)* Lawrence? You in there? This is Kipple Patrick, your mother's friend.

Kip takes the jewel bag from his pocket and tries the door.

It opens wide—on Ora standing far back, dressed for church. She is bolt upright, arms at her sides; and she stares past Kip.

Their meeting unfolds with a measured slowness—no frantic haste but calm deliberation from both.

KIP

Ora—I'm sorry. I was going to leave this. *(Extends the bag)*

Ora shakes her head No, slowly.

KIP

Sell it then; put the money on Lawrence.

ORA

Lawrence got all the money he need.

KIP

Then he must not need what children need—

ORA

Lawrence growing the way his bones *want* to grow—his bones and his good mother's mind. *(Presses a finger against her brow)* Look in here, Kip.

KIP

But when he starts to school and all, the day might come—

ORA

The day might come when God in the sky want to punish you.

She turns back, finds her purse and parasol.

Then she advances on Kip and holds the door as if to shut it behind her.

KIP

You going to late church?

ORA

I'm going anywhere I want to.

She walks out, shuts the door and locks it with a key.

When she has passed Kip and stopped in the yard, she opens the parasol.

Kip stays on the porch.

KIP

Don't get sunburned.

ORA

(Lowering the parasol) Might as well burn now and save on later. I don't want to fry in Hell next to you. *(Begins to leave)*

KIP

This hurts a whole lot worse than I planned.

ORA

It don't hurt me.

KIP

Sarah said different.

ORA

My mother is an old-*timey* soul. She thinks everybody keeping score like her, all the time losing and moaning about it.

KIP

And you're modernistic?

ORA

Call it that if it helps you out. I told you last night—I'm moving, white man. Every part of this body you see is working and sweet, Kip, *sweet.*

KIP

When you say my name, it still sounds sweet.

ORA

Better take your ears to the doctor then.

Kip laughs a short note, then tries to step toward her.

Ora holds up a silent hand to balk him.

KIP

Where's Lawrence now?

ORA

Why you hollering on about Lawrence? You barely mentioned his name before. That child is mine.

KIP

Could I see him a minute?

ORA

If you got X-ray eyes you could. He in Sunday school. Don't you go near him—embarrass him to death. *(Turns to leave)*

KIP

What if I touch you—touch, just touch?

ORA

Everywhere you press, my skin would bruise.

KIP

Was it really that bad?

ORA

Not bad a bit. We were children, Kip. Now we tigers and lions.

KIP

(Half-smiles) You're the tiger, God knows.

ORA

And the tiger's *leaving*.

KIP

Heading up north? Mighty cold up there.

ORA

Cold down *here*, depending on your house. But ease your mind. I won't be sending you no postcards for Kerney to read.

KIP

Let's leave her out. We can live without her.

ORA

You asking me can you live with her and still bump me? *(One low note of laughter)*

KIP

(Waits) Is it cruel as it sounds?

ORA

A lot you do seem to turn out cruel. *(Waits)* No skin off me; I told you I'm leaving.

KIP

Will Lawrence stay?

ORA

Talk to your brain, Kip; it's seriously dumb. You ain't got a particle of right to that child.

KIP

So I tell you goodbye?

ORA

(Meets his eyes and waits a long moment) For the ten-thousandth time—goodbye, thank *Jesus.*

Ora gracefully leaves in languorous strides.

Kip waits a moment, goes to the door and sets the jewel bag down on the sill. Then he leaves too.

4

Two-thirty in the afternoon.

After an enormous meal Kip and Frank are again on the porch. They are both in shirtsleeves, both ties loosened. Their feet are propped on the low railing; and they are rocked back, apparently dozing.

John Bascomb and Kerney walk up, see the sleepers and pause.

John smiles and steps forward.

Kerney holds back till her father pulls gently.

At the bottom of the steps, despite Kerney's frown, John sings a low repeated note.

JOHN

Mi, mi, mi, mi—

Frank wakes instantly and stands.

Kip, exhausted from last night, takes a moment longer but he stands too.

JOHN

Sorry to spoil your much-earned rest.

FRANK

Earned, *nothing*—we were overwhelmed by Sarah's bounty.

JOHN

Walter Parker chloroformed us too. We're walking it off and thought we'd stop by.

FRANK

Fine, step up.

The Bascombs accept and climb the steps. There are only three rockers.

KIP

Kerney, take this chair. *(Indicates his own)*

KERNEY

Rockers make me seasick. I'll sit on the railing.

She sits there, braced against an upright.

John takes the third rocker, and all the men sit.

FRANK

Kerney, you enjoying life?

KERNEY

(Smiles) Struggling to keep my head above water.

JOHN

Kipple, you're clearly thriving.

KIP

I'm swimming for shore.

FRANK

John, you managing to sleep in this heat?

JOHN

I haven't slept a full night in twenty-odd years.

FRANK

All those lads you've lost to the electric chair?

JOHN

(Laughs) More like the ones I got off, scot-free—running loose out here, strangling their kin.

KIP

There's a few I wouldn't mind strangling today.

Looks of incredulity from all, especially Kerney.

FRANK

I very much doubt you mean that, son.

KIP

(Smiles) Not more than once every third or fourth Sunday.

JOHN

You could always hire me right now, Kip. I'll meet you at whatever jail you land in.

Kip nods, smiling, but the unexpected tack has puzzled all four.

Silence spreads and grows uneasy. All hide their feelings in slow responses to the heat—fanning themselves, arranging their clothes.

At last Kerney can bear it no longer and rushes in.

KERNEY

I just figured how to tell when you're grown. *(All turn to listen)* You're grown when you notice the heat. All through my childhood, you grownups were moaning and hunting a breeze. I thought you were crazy. I just played harder and— *(Feeling conspicuous she trails off)*

JOHN

Welcome to the human race—humans get hot.

FRANK

One more reason for not growing up.

Kip rises, finds a palm-leaf fan and hands it to Kerney.

KIP

It's a blessing though, our scorching summer. If anybody finds a way to cool houses, every damned Yankee on the face of the globe will want a share of our peaceful swamp.

JOHN

Start counting, Kip. There are theaters down in Raleigh right now with just such equipment.

KIP

Don't we know it! Our old-maid cousin Lettie Roberts spends all summer at the State Theater, enjoying the breeze and crocheting in the dark. Gets her Christmas presents made by Labor Day.

FRANK

We've got trunks full of Lettie's work—doilies, potholders, indescribables. About as much use as a cement necktie. *(Pronounced CE-ment)*

KERNEY

Like poor Miss Lettie— *(Suddenly embarrassed)*

FRANK

(Smiles but raises a hushing finger) I doubt Lettie knows. She's one busy soul.

Silence spreads again. In a normal visit, such pauses would go unnoticed. But Kerney's unease tilts the visit off stride. Finally—

KERNEY

Kip, I've talked to my father.

Kip is intrigued and abashed. Silence resumes. None of this can be rushed for comedy.

JOHN

Frank, I trust you're apprised of what's befalling us?

FRANK

That these two sprouts enjoy one another?

JOHN

So much so, they plan to flee south.

Kip and Kerney are humiliated.

Frank is baffled and looks to the children.

KIP

Mr. Bascomb, I think you've jumped a few steps.

KERNEY

Pa, you've ruined it.

JOHN

(Laughs) My lord, sweetheart—that's nothing special. I've ruined my life and all those adjacent.

FRANK

(Smiling now) Everybody's breathing—

Kerney is genuinely disturbed. She slips off the railing and faces out, away from the men. Through the following she glances back at them occasionally; she moves as far as the steps, even the white rock.

KERNEY

I'm definitely *not* supposed to be here. I ought to be cool in some theater, crocheting hard and waiting for the man fate has in store. I've not failed to notice how many fine girls wait sixty years and then croak single in a nephew's back room, on charity. That would suit me fine—if I had something grand to do meanwhile, like tall white sculpture or fine true poems that'd have people bawling and set them straight. But I'm not that smart. *(Back at the steps, waits)* Mr. Patrick if all this is coming at you from the blue and you keel over, then excuse me.

FRANK

Kerney, believe me—my life is not threatened by any of this. I know Kip loves you and has asked for your hand.

KERNEY

(Waits) My "hand"—if I could just unplug it and turn it over, things would sure-God be a lot easier for all. But being me, I've got to go through it the hardest way, with all the human beings involved hanging on for dear life and some falling off—

KIP

(Gently) This really is your and my business. Why worry our fathers?

She has no ready answer but seems relieved.

FRANK

Easy, son. The lady's barely started.

Kerney looks to her father.

JOHN

(Slowly nods) Go right on, sweetheart. Get it out of your system.

KERNEY

Kip, I'm inventing a whole new procedure. But in a town as small as this, everybody knows we're testing each other. So ever since we parted last night, I've felt like we ought to sit down now with our two best people and think this through the only right way—if there *is* a way.

KIP

(Slowly) Long as everybody knows we're no way bound by majority rule.

JOHN

Absolutely.

FRANK

Agreed.

They all look to Kerney.

She returns to the porch and sits on the railing, though farther from the men.

KERNEY

I'm scared as hell—excuse me. *(Waits)* See, Kip and I know everything but my answer. He thinks he loves me and I do him. Neither one of us loves all the other one's past; we're working on that. *(Kip tries to hush her with a secret look; she nods and continues)* But see, not having a mother to watch, I got me a powerful taste for freedom and owing nobody—nothing—never. Then I woke up at sixteen and finally heard what the world was saying—I was a girl and must act according. That meant being smart as an infantry general but keeping it the darkest secret in town. So I've toed the line through more than one beau, as they steamed up and offered me diamonds—this is not a brag. It was easy to laugh out loud in their faces. But here came Kip; Kip turned out different— *(Waits, uncertain)*

FRANK

He certainly claims as much for you.

JOHN

A wife and mother needs far more mind than any general.

KERNEY

(Waits) I can thank you both but— *(She is nearer to tears than she has been in weeks)* My mother came— *(Waits)* See, I've been thinking this through so much, my dead mother came in a dream last night. She's worried sick at my tacky clothes and how unready I am for a wedding.

FRANK

Clothes are the last thing you need for a wedding.

JOHN

(Smiles) Frank remember yourself!

FRANK

Excuse me, Kerney. Finish your dream.

With some effort Kerney stands and goes to her father's side. She lays her right hand firmly on his shoulder and faces Frank.

KERNEY

I may soon ask for your son's hand.

Amazed, Kip rises. Then quickly calm, he stands behind Frank.

KERNEY

If I'm to lay down my old dream of being the first white-lady-liontamer, then at least let me take the yoke in style. *(Waits, then launches a dazzling grin)* If I take it—*if.*

KIP

(Quietly to Frank, with a hand on his shoulder) You know I asked for her.

FRANK

(Takes his son's hand but speaks to Kerney) We wait with high hopes—no charge whatever.

KERNEY

(Shakes her head firmly No) I *mean* to pay. If I see my way clear to take Kip's offer, I'll pay him back with my whole life. And we'll both pay you some fraction of all you've sacrificed for us.

JOHN

Darling, that's noble but I'm sure Frank joins me—forget - about - us.

FRANK

Absolute amen.

JOHN

Now about this elopement. Let's talk that through.

KERNEY

(Beginning to wander again) Let's don't. The rest is just me, saying yes or no. *(Waits)* I could flip a coin.

KIP

Is it really that easy? Take the time you need.

KERNEY

But tonight we'll have that big moon again, when my eyes turn green. And *easy*? It's the hardest thing I've had to do since we buried Mother.

KIP

Am I truly that painful a gent to know?

KERNEY

(Waits, then in earnest) So far.

KIP

(Oblivious now to the fathers) Is it that old business?

KERNEY

That *is* on the list.

KIP

Burn the list; I'll eat the ashes.

Suddenly Sarah stands at the screen door, ready to leave, with her sun hat on.

No one yet sees her.

JOHN

Is this a matter we should all consider?

KERNEY

This is private mess.

KIP

And buried now—deep.

FRANK

(Half-whispered to Kip) I fervently hope—

Kip nods in silence.

Sarah has stayed behind the screen door; now she taps lightly on the frame. Though she keeps a dignified courtesy, her memory of last night still clouds her face. She never smiles.

SARAH

I'll be getting on home, Mr. Frank.

FRANK

Not on foot, in this heat.

SARAH

You talk to your company.

FRANK

(Rising) I wouldn't force my worst enemy to walk on a day hot as this, and you're my old friend.

SARAH

Thank you, sir. Well, goodbye to all.

JOHN AND KERNEY

(Separately) Same to you, Sarah. Goodbye.

KIP

(Also to Sarah) I thanked you in my church prayers today.

SARAH

(A short wait, unsmiling) I'm bound to be glad.

KIP

Now you pray for *me.* I'm weak as a kitten.

SARAH

I hadn't stopped yet and I got you this far.

FRANK

Sarah Gavin's prayers get *results.*

SARAH

God know my voice. He heard it so much, He answer me just to shut me up. *(Suddenly laughs, a deep inner laugh from calm wells; then turns and heads for the back door)*

FRANK

This won't take but twenty minutes. Kip, see if our friends wouldn't like a glass of something.

KIP

(Rising also) Gladly—tea, lemonade, coffee, stronger po - ta - tions?

JOHN

(Rising) I'll ride with you, Frank. We can loop on past my mother's homeplace. I heard it nearly burned last week.

FRANK

There was a fire but the last time I drove by, the house was still full of blue-black young uns.

JOHN

They *are* a people that thrives on pain. By the year two thousand, they'll rule the Earth.

Kip and Kerney look to one another, puzzled.

Both fathers mean their words in earnest.

FRANK

And when they rule, I hope they recall I drove Sarah home, in sun or snow. You get Walter to speak a word for you.

JOHN

Walter will govern the first black state. They'll elect him just to get a little peace—like God and Sarah's prayers. The question is, will God let *us* live?

FRANK

Of course not; we know it. We'll be flung against a wall and machine-gunned down by Judgment Day evening.

John nods assent.

KERNEY

Pa, don't joke—you don't believe that.

KIP

I do, every word.

JOHN

(To Kerney) Does it take the village agnostic to remind you what St. Paul says? *(Pauses to remember)*

KIP

(In the pause, lines it out gravely) "Be not deceived. God is not mocked. For as a man soweth, so shall he also reap."

Kerney searches Kip's face.

But Kip nods earnestly.

Frank and then John move toward the yard.

JOHN

You children be here when we get back?

The fathers continue walking through the next exchanges.

KERNEY

As opposed to South Carolina, you mean? Go cool yourself. Strip buck-naked and swim in the quarry. I know a few girls that go out there. They're trashy but warm.

KIP

Take the snakebite kit. There's girls *and* snakes.

FRANK

At no time in history have snakes and girls ever not been together.

KERNEY

Whoa, Mr. Bascomb!

The fathers disappear.

KIP

(Calls to them) We'll be right here.

FRANK

(From off) I almost hope you won't.

KIP

(To Kerney) Where did that come from?

KERNEY

The depths of a father's endless love.

Kip is puzzled by that and mimes the word "What?"

But when she does not answer, he steps to where she sits on the railing, stopping two feet short of touch.

From here to the end, they are deferential, even tender, with one another; but they are grave—no coyness or levity. More than ever they feel the weight of Ora and Lawrence in their present transaction.

KIP

What made you move this far, this fast?

KERNEY

I haven't moved.

KIP

But you give grounds for hope.

KERNEY

You don't hate me yet?

KIP

(Waits) Not yet.

KERNEY

Kip, that dream last night was *strong*. Mother was truly there, in my room. She went to your mother. And they—

Tears ambush her.

When Kip moves to hold her, she waves him back.

He sits in the nearest rocker, below her.

KERNEY

(Carefully) See, I was barely in sight of womanhood when Mother died. So she never taught me about the deep things—love and freedom and trusting people. I've hurt lots of people.

KIP

Not me, never me.

KERNEY

You forget it now because I'm here. If we do finally spend years together, it'll flood back over you—all my meanness, my mystifications, just to be a crossroads Cleopatra.

KIP

If that time comes, you'll have done so much good, the past will seem silly.

KERNEY

(Waits) Kip, that *was* my mother, not a dream. It was something else, like a serious dance God sent me to watch.

KIP

What was in it beside your clothes?

KERNEY

Like I said, *your* mother. She was at your house, and my mother hugged her and borrowed my whole trousseau and—

KIP

Wait. *(Almost remembers his own dream)* Did they stop a minute and look at me?

KERNEY

(Nods) You were fast asleep but my mother touched you.

KIP

(Waits, shakes his head) Whatever I saw is gone. Did my mother speak.

KERNEY

Didn't need words. They both looked fine.

KIP

I don't have a clear recollection of her face. And her voice—God, her voice is so far gone, I'd give a month's pay to hear it again.

KERNEY

(Calmly) Ora was here.

KIP

No, not so.

KERNEY

In the dream, Kip. Ora sat in the midst of everything else and watched all everybody did and felt till—

KIP

Ora is *stopped*, in my life at least.

Kip puts an arm on Kerney's shoulder. With the free hand he tries to hush her mouth.

But she slips off the railing, runs down the steps and stops to look back. Then she returns as far as the steps and speaks with quiet fervor.

KERNEY

There's a child involved, with your eyes and hair.

KIP

Ora swears he's not mine.

KERNEY

What if he knocks on the door in ten years and asks for his father? What are my instructions?

KIP

That's your old meanness—

KERNEY

(Shakes her head) It's a serious question.

Kip moves toward the steps.

Kerney draws back farther.

KIP

(With an equal calm heat) I could have lain upstairs many nights and hurt myself, to the backbone-*quick*, guessing at what exact hot things you were doing that minute with Jeffer Burns and a few other boys that had cars to drive—

KERNEY

My boys were white and free-will agents. I never once leaned on anybody's weakness.

KIP

You sure-God leaned on their feeble brains. Kerney, I'm filthy to the crown of my hair; but I don't go sniffing at your past crimes.

KERNEY

(Waits) Is that the real truth?

KIP

(Raises a hand) It's one of the rare good traits of my heart—I cancel the past.

KERNEY

(Waits) I think you truly believe yourself, but I think you're lying. *(A sudden discovery)* Even our mothers—in my dream—tried to shame Ora Lee. I can't have that.

She stands still a moment more, then turns to walk home.

Kip follows a few steps.

KIP

No, God. *No.*

Kerney stops and faces him but does not return.

KIP

This is not what we want.

KERNEY

It hurts too much—me and you, too many others. Every time we're in hailing distance, we wind up clawing each other to tears. Now we cut on Ora and that little boy— *(Waits)* Maybe two orphans ought not to mate.

KIP

(He suddenly smiles) Don't that sound tragic?

KERNEY

Don't pat my head.

KIP

I wish I could hold it, this instant for good, and shield your mind from the world *and* from you. You want this Earth to be Heaven too. It ain't even scheduled to be Heaven soon.

KERNEY

(Calming too) Now listen to the Wise One.

KIP

(Extends his hands) I am wise, hon. Look at all these wounds. Hell, I'm two years older.

Kerney will not move.

KIP

I can barely stand this. *(Waits)* You feel too strong, like the strong North Pole; and I'm the iron needle. If you don't mean to leave, at least turn your back.

Kerney slowly obeys.

KIP

(Waits) I still feel you, strong.

Slowly Kerney faces around again.

KERNEY

It's not me you feel.

KIP

Who in God's name else?

KERNEY

You're a lonesome man.

KIP

Which makes you a woman. And we're aging fast. From where I stand, I don't see a crowd of men vowing to give you what I vow.

Entirely serious, Kerney looks around her; then faces Kip again.

KERNEY

Say it once more.

KIP

Lord, you've got it by memory.

KERNEY

It's strange to me—so strange I lose it.

KIP

I vow to cherish you long as I live. I'll set you far above anyone else. And all I've got—my body and mind—will be yours only till we have children that need our care.

KERNEY

Our fathers included—in your vow, I mean.

KIP

(Nods firmly) But nobody else.

Kerney thinks, then faces him frankly.

KERNEY

Would we leave tonight?

KIP

I've got Monday off.

KERNEY

Do we wait for them or just leave a message?

KIP

Let's vote, here and now.

KERNEY

We might cancel each other.

KIP

The *moon* might crack. Kip Patrick might root to the ground, waiting here.

Kerney slowly nods, shuts her eyes, bows her head for one long moment, then points to the white rock in the center where Ora sat throughout the dream. From now till the last line, she remains unsure of her final choice.

KERNEY

Will you meet me there?

KIP

I can surely try.

Kerney seems to lose nerve and looks toward home. But she waits another moment and silently steps to the rock.

Kip joins her there, an arm's reach between them. But they do not touch.

It may be possible to strengthen the memory of Ora by beginning, low, some black instrumental music of the time—jazz or swing.

KIP

You glad?

KERNEY

(Waits) Not yet, maybe headed there.

KIP

So's Kipple, I'm almost ready to vow. *(Waits)* Lean toward me.

KERNEY

Toward you, not *on* you?

KIP

Hoping I knew you, I said it that way. *(Waits)* Are we leaving now?

KERNEY

How about sundown? We can get fresh clothes and be on the road before moonrise.

KIP

My trousseau's on me, right this minute. And why moonrise?

KERNEY

So I'll be well-dressed but locked in a car when that light strikes me.

Kerney draws back a little, suddenly fearful. She hugs her shoulders, shivers and repeats her growl from the night before. Then she moves a step back nearer Kip.

KIP

(Shivers also) Is it maybe a deal?

KERNEY

Maybe—for the worse?

KIP

I'm praying for strength.

KERNEY

That's what it'll take.

KIP

Lady, you'll be amazed.

KERNEY

You too. I *vow.*

So Kip offers her both his hands.

When Kerney accepts them, Kip's arms move round her.

Hers go to Kip's waist.

Slowly they lean toward one another like a pair of Pisan towers. When they meet, they smile and slowly embrace.

ABOUT THE AUTHOR

Reynolds Price was born in Macon, North Carolina in 1933. Reared and educated in the public schools of his native state, he earned an A.B. *summa cum laude* from Duke University. In 1955 he traveled as a Rhodes Scholar to Merton College, Oxford University, to study English literature. After three years, and the B. Litt. degree, he returned to Duke where he continues to teach as James B. Duke Professor of English.

In 1962 his novel *A Long and Happy Life* appeared. It received the William Faulkner Award for a notable first novel and has never been out of print. Since, he has published other novels—*Blue Calhoun* (1992) was the ninth—and in 1986 his *Kate Vaiden* received the National Book Critics Circle Award. He has also published volumes of stories, poems, plays, essays, translations from the Bible, a memoir *Clear Pictures*; and he has written for the screen, for television and the texts for songs. His television play *Private Contentment* was commissioned by *American Playhouse* and appeared in its premiere season. His trilogy of plays *New Music* premiered at the Cleveland Play House in 1989; and its three plays have been produced throughout the country. In 1993 his *Collected Stories*, the work of five decades, will appear.

He is a member of the American Academy of Arts and Letters, and his books have appeared in sixteen languages.